INTERNSHIP PROGRAMS
IN
EDUCATIONAL ADMINISTRATION

A Guide to Preparing
Educational Leaders

INTERNSHIP PROGRAMS
IN
EDUCATIONAL ADMINISTRATION

A Guide to Preparing
Educational Leaders

MIKE M. MILSTEIN
BETTYE M. BOBROFF
L. NAN RESTINE

TEACHERS
COLLEGE
PRESS

Teachers College, Columbia University
New York and London

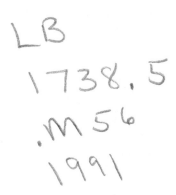

Published by Teachers College Press, 1234 Amsterdam Avenue, New York, NY 10027

Milstein, Mike M.
    Internship programs in educational administration: a guide to preparing educational leaders / Mike M. Milstein, Bettye M. Bobroff, L. Nan Restine.
        p.   cm.
    Includes bibliographical references (p.) and index.
    ISBN 0-8077-3080-7 (alk. paper). — ISBN 0-8077-3079-3 (pbk. : alk. paper)
    1. School administrators—Training of—United States.   2. School management and organi-zation—Study and teaching (Internship)—United States.   3. Internship programs—United States.   I. Bobroff, Bettye M.   II. Restine, L. Nan.   III. Title.
LB1738.5.M56   1991
370'.7'7—dc20   91-10170

ISBN 0-8077-3080-7
ISBN 0-8077-3079-3 (pbk.)

Printed on acid-free paper
Manufactured in the United States of America

98 97 96 95 94 93 92 91 8 7 6 5 4 3 2 1

Contents

Foreword

FOR MORE THAN FORTY YEARS, internship has been little emphasized as a developmental activity for aspiring school leaders. While research is meager on the question of whether internships affect the outcomes needed for effective school leadership, universities and colleges have continued to include the experience as a part of preparation for certification and/or licensing.

Current data that project the future staffing needs of our nation's schools indicate that vast numbers of school principals will soon be eligible for retirement. Important questions raised by reports on school administration concern who will fill those vacancies and how candidates should be prepared to provide leadership in a society that is constantly changing. Numerous educators are calling for the preparation of principals through experiential learning opportunities, including internships and greater interaction with university faculty and with practicing school administrators.

Milstein, Bobroff, and Restine have responded to the challenges issued by national commissions, state departments of education, and school districts by developing alternative procedures for preparing educational leaders for the twenty-first century. This book provides university faculty and school administrators with the know-how to ensure that interns gain both a theoretical knowledge of school administration and the practical skills necessary to function effectively as administrators.

Interns need to regularly test their ability to place theoretical and textbook learnings into practice and learn from the consequences. The experiences provided for in this book are designed to prepare the candidates so that in their first position as a practicing administrator, they will have an understanding of the operation of a school and be able to exert a style of leadership in the school and community beyond that currently in vogue.

Internship programs that engage universities and school districts as partners can integrate the practical knowledge of practicing administrators into the academic experiences provided by the university. The practicalities of establishing, maintaining, and evaluating an internship program are to be found in this book. Implementation is left to the reader.

Donn W. Gresso
Vice President
The Danforth Foundation

Preface

THE INTENT OF THIS BOOK is to provide guidance for the development, implementation, management, and evaluation of effective internship programs. As such, it is intended to be used as a handbook, a textbook, and a general resource book for four groups:

1. *Those who are responsible for developing and conducting internship programs,* whether within universities or school districts, at the school-site level, or in the central office.
2. *Those who participate as interns.* The book includes practical exercises, a variety of criteria, and checklists, as well as basic knowledge, that should make it useful for internship seminars and as a guidebook for site-based activities.
3. *Those who supervise interns' site activities.* These professionals can benefit from clarification of expectations, both of the interns and of supervisors/mentors.
4. *Those who are responsible for developing policies for internship activities in school districts.* These individuals shoulder the responsibility for identifying, selecting, and preparing tomorrow's district leaders. The book should help them with these tasks and prepare them to work cooperatively with university personnel in the effort.

While the book may be used by any of these groups, we believe it is a resource that can bring together all internship aspects in a more holistic and effective manner. That is, it can be used to guide the development or modification of internship programs, provide for a coherent set of internship activities as students go through the experience, evaluate the results of the effort, and, subsequently, promote more effective strategies for moving individuals from the status of novice and into educational leadership roles.

The book is concerned with *people* and *programs.* The intent regarding people is to promote introspection, decisions to take risks and grow, and opportunities to assess progress toward personal and professional goals. The intent regarding programs is to encourage the development and implementation of a comprehensive set of activities and experiences that are likely to challenge participants in ways that many internship programs presently neglect. In particular, programs should blend useful knowledge with skills and personal development opportunities that promote the leadership capacities of all participants—staff, faculty, interns and site administrators.

Readers are encouraged to apply the ideas and suggestions contained in the book in ways that best fit their own particular settings and situations. Although there should be some universal expectations, such as the provision of knowledge and skills and opportunities for their application, we realize that each situation will be unique. As such, it is important that the planning, implementation, and management of internship programs reflect these differences.

In this regard, the book can be of assistance to internship programs sponsored by educational administration departments in universities, to school districts that choose to design their own internship programs, and to university–school district partnerships that seek to develop cooperatively conducted internship programs. In fact, the advantages and disadvantages of these alternative arrangements are explored in the book.

For the sake of coherence, the information included in the book is presented from the vantage point of university-based internship program governance and management. Readers are encouraged to view the ideas presented as universally relevant, but to interpret them as applied to their own particular situations.

The book begins with an introduction that provides a frame of reference for exploring the demands for effective internship programs and depicting the approach and biases of the authors.

Part I, Developing and Implementing the Internship Program, is composed of four chapters. Chapter 2 focuses on the various groups involved in the program: the internship director and staff, university faculty members, interns, field supervisors, and site administrators. Criteria for selection of these participants are discussed in this chapter. Chapter 3 explores requirements that should be given serious consideration in the development of programs that bring theory and practice together in effective ways. The focus is on purposes, responsibilities, and key design elements. Chapter 4 provides useful ways of thinking about the knowledge that should be explored, how it should be delivered (courses, internship seminars, and field-site observations and experiences), and who can best deliver it. Chapter 5 focuses on the partnership that is required for the program to have its intended outcomes. The partnership provides advantages for all participants, but should not be taken for granted. To work well, it should be based on clear understandings and expectations as well as upon opportunities for negotiation and clarification.

Part II, Follow-Up, includes two chapters. Chapter 6 suggests ways of helping interns move from the world of preparation to the world of work. It includes examination of networking, career planning, job searching, and ways of successfully applying for administrative positions. Chapter 7 discusses the importance of evaluating the interns and the program and provides suggestions for going about it. It highlights the topical areas that should be included in the evaluation of interns and the program and suggests a variety of methodological approaches that should be considered in the effort. With evaluation we come full circle; that is, with the knowledge gained from evaluation efforts, we are in a good position to know what, if any, modifications are required to assure a clinical capacity that will meet the needs of our schools and provide interns with opportunities for personal and professional growth.

The book closes with an epilogue and a collection of supplemental materials. The epilogue looks to the future and the challenges that will confront those who are charged with the responsibility of preparing tomorrow's educational leaders. The appendices, composed of supplementary materials, have been included to provide readers with ideas and information that expand on the contents of the chapter. Included are guidelines related to mentoring and problem project development; professional associations to contact for information (e.g., about internship programs and career placement); suggested survey and evaluation forms; (for new interns, intern alumni, and site administrators); and brief scenarios that can be used in internship seminars to stimulate discussion about administrative situations.

The book is intended to encourage interactive learning. Readers will find exercises in most chapters that are aimed at helping them personalize learnings and translate general suggestions to meet their particular needs. In this regard, readers are also encouraged to turn to the appendices, which contain a variety of examples of approaches and strategies that are introduced in the chapters.

The ideas expressed here bring together much of the best that is presently being explored within more innovative internship programs. We believe they will help program designers, interns, field supervisors, and site administrators create and maintain excellent internship programs. To the extent that this occurs, our purposes will have been well served.

INTERNSHIP PROGRAMS IN EDUCATIONAL ADMINISTRATION

A Guide to Preparing Educational Leaders

CHAPTER 1

Introduction: The Increasing Demand for Administrative Internship Programs

ONE PREDICTABLE RESULT of the educational reform movement has been a call for increased efficiency and effectiveness of the educational enterprise. Inevitably, this has had an impact on the way we prepare educational leaders. Those involved in such preparation are being challenged to modify their programs and, in some cases, to develop clinical experiences that support this need.

This book reflects the growing sense of urgency about the way our school leaders are being prepared. This chapter explores the educational reform movement and the emerging consensus that the implementation of needed educational reforms requires changes in the training of the school administrators who must facilitate them. It describes the intent and biases of the book and suggests ways that readers might use it to improve their planning, management, and evaluation of internship programs.

REFORM AND LEADERSHIP

Beginning with the release of *A Nation at Risk* (National Commission on Excellence in Education, 1983), the 1980s witnessed an unprecedented call for educational reform. Dissatisfaction with our schools' performance (e.g., declining SAT scores, business and industry's concern about lack of worker literacy, negative comparisons of U.S. students' achievement with that of students from other countries) mounted over the decade. This dissatisfaction soon spread from federal government reports to state investigations, reports by prestigious private organizations such as the Carnegie Foundation (Boyer, 1983), and studies from within the profession itself (e.g., Goodlad, 1983).

Duttweiler (1988) notes that the initial wave of reform called for "top-

1

down" mandates to raise standards and ensure accountability. As might be expected, there has been much resistance by school boards, administrators, and teachers to reform by legislation. This is because top-down policy making often fails to take local dynamics into account and rarely provides sufficient resources to implement intended reforms.

As a result of this resistance, a second wave of reform has followed, urging "bottom-up" changes that emanate from the local level. Currently, bottom-up reforms call for such things as school-based budgeting and management, restructuring, professional development schools, and teacher empowerment. Such reforms will require significant changes in how our schools and school districts are governed and led. Many school districts are exploring ways of moving toward these changes.

However, rhetoric alone will not move our schools in these directions. "The greatest barriers to school improvements are within the school system. . . . Insiders are predisposed to defend the status quo either because they believe in it or because they have been trained in ways that blind them to other possibilities" (Wayson, Mitchell, Pinell, & Landis, 1988, p. 19).

The implementation of needed reforms is highly dependent on efforts by site-based administrators who have the vision, beliefs, abilities, and energy required to lead others toward shared objectives. In fact, the literature on educational effectiveness and school excellence (e.g., Edmonds, 1979; Joyce, Hersh, & McKibbin, 1983; Lieberman & Miller, 1984; Mangieri, 1985; Rouche & Baker, 1986; Spady & Marx, 1984) clearly points to the key role of educational administrators in such efforts.

Educational administrators, particularly those at the school site, are at the center of the action. As such, they are in a position to have a major impact on school improvement. Depending on how they choose to lead, that impact can range from highly detrimental to highly supportive. Given the importance of their role, the critical nature of leader preparation and selection cannot be overemphasized.

PREPARATION OF EDUCATIONAL ADMINISTRATORS: A BRIEF HISTORICAL PERSPECTIVE

The preparation of educational administrators has long been an accepted activity of colleges of education, especially in our comprehensive universities (e.g., Allison, 1989). During the first half of the twentieth century this responsibility was typically held by retired school administrators who joined colleges of education and shared their experiences with novices. Despite the inherent shortcomings in this approach, at least those entering the field were learning from highly experienced administrators.

The emphasis of training programs changed significantly after the late 1950s, when private organizations such as the Kellogg Foundation provided support for reform of these programs (National Society for the Study of Education, 1964). Training shifted from retired administrators who told war stories to professors who presented theoretical models from the behavioral sciences. The assumption was that these models could help clarify the world of educational management. The theory movement grew during the 1960s and 1970s, and faculty were selected on the basis of their academic preparation rather than their experience as administrators, with the result being that preparation became further removed from hands-on learning and experiential applications.

While the movement toward theory provided frameworks for understanding, it also created a chasm between the bearers of that theory and those who had to make use of it in practice. For the most part it was assumed that, armed with theory, administrators would be able to make effective use of it to improve their leadership activities. This assumption was and is questionable.

Predictably, educational reformers began to criticize the situation. Even those responsible for the preparation of administrators soon began to join the negative chorus. In fact, the National Commission on Excellence in Educational Administration, which was supported by the body that represents many of the more comprehensive university-based training programs, the University Council for Educational Administration, played a leading role in this criticism. The commission was particularly critical of the practitioner-related elements of preparation programs, which it said were marked by "lack of a definition of good educational leadership . . . lack of collaboration between school districts and universities . . . lack of systematic professional development for school administrators . . . lack of sequence, modern content, and clinical experiences" (1987, pp. xvi–xvii).

It was not long before those receiving this training became skeptical of its utility (e.g., Department of Elementary School Principals, 1968; Griffiths, 1988; Heller, Conway, & Jacobsen, 1988). Murphy and Hallinger (1987) conclude:

> Practitioners have become disillusioned by the failure of university programs to ground training procedures in the realities of the workplace and by their reluctance to treat content viewed as useful by administrators. This disenchantment, in turn, is partially fueling the demand for changes in methods of training school administrators. (p. 252)

Pressures for change in the preparation of educational administrators have increased significantly through the end of the 1980s and the early 1990s. In part these pressures for reform are based on disappointment with the theory movement and the inability or unwillingness of universities to voluntarily modify their approaches to training administrators (Murphy & Hallinger, 1987). However, it also has much to do with overall perceptions of educational conditions. There is growing awareness of the key role of administrators in educational improvement and a realization that too often administrators are not prepared to cope with core technical operations and responsibilities, such as instructional leadership.

THE GROWING ROLE OF CLINICAL EXPERIENCE IN PREPARATION PROGRAMS

Clinical experience is a well-established expectation in the preparation programs of such professions as medicine and law. In fact, the term *internship,* as applied in educational administration, has been borrowed from the field of medicine, where it refers to "the hospital experience required of every M.D. near or at the end of his college preparation program" (Skalski et al., 1987, p. 1).

The impetus for the development of internships in educational administration first emerged in 1947 at a meeting of the newly founded National Conference of Professors of Educational Administration. Only the University of Chicago and the University of Omaha had this requirement in their preparation programs at that time. As a result of the discussions at the meeting, other universities began to explore this activity. In fact, during the next academic year five other universities instituted internship requirements, and by 1950 there were seventeen with such expectations (Wheaton, 1950).

The 1950s witnessed continuing interest in the development of viable internship programs. Most important was the Kellogg Foundation's support of the Cooperative Program in Educational Administration. This program supported eight universities, including Teachers College at Columbia, Harvard, and Ohio State, which committed themselves to examine ways of improving preparation of educational administrators, with particular emphasis on internship activities.

By 1962, the number of universities including internships as part of their programs had climbed to 117 (Hencley, 1963). This trend continued through the 1980s. In a survey conducted by Skalski and associates (1987) to which 252 universities responded, 220 (87%) included an internship, while 32 (13%) did not. The survey also found that, of those responding, 59% required their students to take an internship and 64% reported that state certification required an internship. There was wide variation in expectations, but 165 hours was the average minimum on-site requirement, the norm was for one-semester internships, and the academic credit was normally three or six hours. The number of students enrolled at any one time in an internship experience also varied greatly (from none to 150), with the mean being about 28.

Despite the rapid increase in the number of universities conducting internship programs and the widespread acceptance of this approach, there have been few comprehensive analyses of its impact. In fact, the most recent major effort to do so occurred about three decades ago when the University Council for Educational Administration and the Commission for the Advancement of School Administration sponsored an edited volume (Hencley, 1963) on the subject. A review by Daresh (1987) indicates that little serious analysis has occurred since.

The general impression that exists is that clinical experiences, particularly internships, have been one of the weakest aspects of preparation programs. In fact, many programs still do not require clinical experiences of their students. Further, whether required or not, these experiences tend to be minimally supervised and organized, and there is little prior understanding and agreement about expectations among university personnel, site supervisors, and interns. The result of such benign neglect is predictable:

> Too often field sites are chosen haphazardly and/or are not closely monitored. The potential for interns being constrained to passive observation, being placed in roles which do not fit closely with their career goals, or being used as "go-fers," is great when clear and agreed-upon expectations are not developed. Likewise, campus-based practicums and seminars on a regular basis are rarely available or required and clinical experiences are often isolated from the rest of a students' program flow. Finally, the connecting linkages between on-campus experiences and field-based experiences are rarely adequately developed. (Milstein, 1990, p. 121)

Most preparation programs can be criticized "for not providing the field-based experiences necessary for developing outstanding principals" (Anderson, 1989, p. 56) and other educational leaders. The time has come for us to make greater efforts to provide this important activity.

Intellectual knowledge, in and of itself is not enough. As regards preparation of educational leaders, knowledge has to be balanced with the ability to perform effectively if we expect to improve our schools. Learning, in the context of preparation of educational leaders, takes place most meaningfully when there is opportunity to apply concepts. Our bias is to emphasize active learning over passive learning. The principles that guide our suggestions for the development and implementation of internship programs emanate from this bias. Ultimately we must provide:

a balance between *learning about* and *learning how*, rooted in a solid foundation of *learning why*. In the process, students should have multiple opportunities to demonstrate mastery of those skills and knowledge traditionally required of administrative positions as well as those which have not yet been clearly identified but which may be required in the future. (Milstein, 1990, p. 122)

Internship programs should emphasize leadership as well as management. That is, while they must be concerned with helping the novice learn basic skills and techniques for managing the enterprise, they should also encourage exploration of leadership potential through personal reflection, development of educational platforms/philosophies, promotion of effective interpersonal styles, and a desire for continuing professional development (Daresh, 1988).

Competence in management and leadership are both important ends of preparation programs, and activities should be devoted to helping participants become more skilled at both. Anything less is insufficient, especially during times of rapid change and escalating expectations, both of which are likely to continue in the foreseeable future.

Most professional fields—for example, law, medicine, and business as well as education—provide opportunities for internships. When they are planned with care and when interns are given opportunities to work with exceptional leaders, these clinical experiences can have a positive impact on interns' confidence and their ability to perform as leaders.

It is estimated that about 60% of our current principals will be retiring during the 1990s (Anderson, 1989). This provides both challenges and opportunities. During this decade we will have the chance to reshape the educational leadership of our schools. To do so, however, requires that we first significantly improve the preparation of those who will move into these vacated positions. One major element of that effort has to do with the field-related portion of preparation, particularly the internship experience.

PURPOSES OF INTERNSHIP PROGRAMS

From the literature on internship programs (e.g., Daresh, 1987; Grady, Layton, & Bohling-Philipi, 1988; LaPlant, 1988; Short & Ashbaugh, 1988; Skalski et al., 1987); several purposes emerge that provide justification for administrative internship programs. The core purpose is to assure the leadership required to support our schools. Internships can link intellectual competence with outstanding performance, if thoughtfully planned and conducted in stimulating settings. Specific purposes can be viewed from the vantage points of students, school districts, and the university.

Purposes for Students

Inherent in the mission of administrative preparation programs is the need for internships or field experiences. Most school administrators and university faculty members agree that internships should constitute a significant part of future administrators' preparation. The study of administrative areas, observation of administrators in action ("shadowing"), participatory activities, and specific administrative assignments offer opportunities for interns to internalize and employ administrative skills learned during their graduate coursework.

What this refers to is, in Daresh's (1988) terms, "professional formation wherein administrative candidates put together learning acquired in the field and in the classroom and also their own values and priorities to form more holistic and personal understandings of educational leadership" (p. 14). Schön refers to this as "knowing-in-practice" or "reflection-in-action"; that is, "on the spot surfacing, criticizing, restructuring, and testing of intuitive understandings of experienced phenomena" (1984, p. 42).

Students need opportunities to apply knowledge gained from their university coursework. School systems are placing a higher priority on identifying candidates who have completed quality programs that include on-the-job learning experiences. As a result of participating in an internship program, students can determine whether they have the ability and desire to function as administrators. It is far better to discover that these are lacking during an internship experience than to realize it after accepting an administrative position from which it is psychologically very difficult to return to a classroom position.

Purposes for School Districts

Several benefits can accrue to school districts that are involved in internship programs and that encourage their staff members to participate in them. First, it provides them with opportunities to encourage involvement of high-quality teachers who have the potential to become excellent administrators. Second, by participating in the planning and designing of internship programs, school districts enhance the likelihood that interns will be involved in meaningful and high-caliber learning experiences. Third, school district cooperation assures that interns will have unique opportunities to observe administrators at work and thus gain a more comprehensive view of administrative roles, even if they eventually decide to return to classroom situations. Finally, and perhaps most important, by participating actively, school districts have the advantage of observing and evaluating interns' performance in actual work situations prior to appointing them to administrative positions.

Purposes for Universities

Universities also benefit from including internships or other field-based experiences in their programs for potential administrators. As the National Commission on Excellence in Educational Administration (1987) notes:

> Administrator preparation programs should be like those in professional schools which emphasize theoretical and clinical knowledge, applied research, and supervised practice. . . . The Commission argues that the logic of professional preparation, which introduces students to theory and research and then guides them into the world of practice, is well-suited for the important work of school administration. The necessary close working relationship between the university and the world of practice will benefit the quality of research and the quality of administrator preparation. In addition, public interests are served by the fact that administrators have studied school administration in the university and have been mentored by a team of research and clinical professors prior to independent practice. (p. 20)

CLEAR AND APPROPRIATE PURPOSES set the parameters and the intent for internship programs. Equally important, if students, school system leaders, and university faculty participate in the development of programs, it is more likely that broad-based support or "ownership" will be created and maintained.

PART I

Developing and Implementing the Internship Program

CHAPTER 2

Recruitment and Selection of Participants

THE PROCEDURES USED for the recruitment and selection of participants in an administrative internship program and the degree of forethought, based on well-established principles regarding what constitutes effective leadership, have direct implications for developing quality programs. Simply "handing the keys" to those who have fulfilled nebulous requirements is not acceptable: The responsibility placed on current and future educational administrators demands that those selected for these roles be those with the potential for superior leadership. Today's educational leaders are being confronted with high expectations and increasing demands for improved education. Leadership tasks have become more complex as technological changes and sociological trends have placed greater demands on educational systems.

As such, the population of students in administrative preparation programs must possess more than marginal interest and talent. Likewise, those responsible for the content and delivery of the program must be increasingly better informed, be positive role models, and desire to create the best possible learning situations for interns.

The quality of participants is much too important to be left to chance. The selection and recruitment of participants is the most critical element in an internship program. The reputation of programs and their impact on the educational community as a whole are directly related to the quality of those participating in preparation programs. They must be quality individuals able to interact positively and effectively with multiple constituencies. Proactive recruitment for all the role players is imperative and should be based on well-conceived expectations for each role.

How is it possible to be sure that those recruited and selected as interns and supervisors are indeed the most able? What types of characteristics deserve attention? How are these characteristics related to the overall objectives of the program? How can these characteristics be assessed? By whom?

This chapter discusses important considerations for the selection of participants in internship programs. It is suggested that universities and school districts collaborate in assessing personal and professional characteristics for the program director, site administrators, field supervisors, and administrative interns. This chapter will first explore criteria of leadership that apply to all participants. These criteria will then be examined with respect to each particular role, with suggested procedures for recruitment and selection.

COMMON SELECTION CRITERIA ACROSS ROLE GROUPS

The fundamental theme of an educational administration internship program is leadership. As such, the criteria established for the selection of participants should focus on attributes that exemplify leadership. In addition, the procedures used for selection and recruitment should emulate valued leadership approaches.

Personal Characteristics of Leaders

All participants should maintain a high degree and intensity of vision. They should be active agents for change. As Kouzes and Posner (1987) state:

> The root origin of the word *lead* is a word meaning "to go." This root origin denotes travel from one place to another. In this sense, leaders are pioneers. By comparison, the root origin of *manage* is a word meaning "hand." Managing seems to connote "handling" things. A major difference can be found in what it means to handle things and what it means to go places. The unique reason for having leaders—their differentiating function—is to move us forward. (pp. 32–33)

Leaders may come in all shapes and sizes, but they share some common characteristics. According to Bennis (1989), the basic characteristics that distinguish leaders from managers include:

- *A guiding vision:* Leaders must have clear ideas, both personally and professionally, about where they and the organization are going and why.
- *Passion:* The leader is able to communicate hope, inspiration, and a course for action. This ingredient is basically a love of life and a commitment to improving situations for self and others.
- *Integrity:* The essential elements of integrity include self-knowledge, candor, and maturity. Self-knowledge includes knowledge of personal assets as well as deficits and honesty in recognizing the difference. Candor forms the basis of this honesty. The quality of maturity means *doing* what one wishes others to do, not simply *telling* them to do it.

• *Trustworthiness:* Trust refers to the level of confidence felt for one by others. It is the basis of the belief that the convictions of those in a position of guardianship are worthy of support. This trust, which must be earned, is most instrumental in the leader's ability to function.
• *Curiosity and daring:* Curiosity and daring involve taking risks and learning from adversity, the willingness to experiment and attempt new things.

Taken together, these criteria differentiate leaders from managers, according to Bennis. He further explicates these differences as shown in Figure 2.1.

The leadership column reflects the qualities of finding problems (identifying those which are not always clearly defined) as well solving them, of being an educator rather than a trainer. The management column reflects concern with the short run, profit maximizing, and the bottom line (a perspective encouraged by business schools).

With this in mind, it is important to note that the conceptualization of educational administration by those participating in the design and conduct of internship programs influences those selected to serve in specific capacities. Accordingly, we must learn to devise ways in which to assess those characteristics deemed most relevant.

In addition, it is critical to include among the selection criteria the capacity for *mentoring.* Many definitions of mentoring exist, from adviser, to advocate, to tutor, to supervisor. The classical definition suggests that the mentor is emotionally involved in guiding and influencing the protégé(e)'s personal as well as professional life (Muse, Wasden, & Thomas, 1988). Much

FIGURE 2.1: A Comparison of the Characteristics of Leaders and Managers

LEADERS	MANAGERS
Innovate	Administer
Are Original	Are Copies
Develop	Maintain
Focus on People	Focus on Structure
Inspire Trust	Rely on Control
Have a Long-range Perspective	Have a Short-range Perspective
Ask What and Why	Ask How and When
Focus on the Horizon	Focus on the Bottom Line
Originate	Imitate
Are Their Own Person	Are "Good Soldiers"
Do the Right Thing	Do Things Right
Challenge the Status Quo	Accept the Status Quo

research attests to the fact that mentoring relationships have a profound influence on the success and career development of new and aspiring members of a profession (Bova & Phillips, 1984; Phillips-Jones, 1983; Roche, 1979). Those who are benefited by mentoring are more likely to serve in this capacity for others and thus perpetuate this legacy as part of the organizational culture.

The selection of professionals with the capacity for mentoring alleviates the isolation that aspiring or novice administrators may sense. In this way, networking is enhanced and communication channels among peers and colleagues are developed. A willingness to learn about mentoring and a commitment to preparing future educational administrators should be viewed as paramount in the selection and recruitment of participants. Information and guidelines concerning mentoring are found in Appendix A.

Assessing the Leadership of All Participants

In developing a successful internship program, the selection of all participants may generally be based on the categories of personal attributes, professional reputation, professional experiences, and academic preparation. Prior to establishing criteria for recruitment and selection, program planners should determine how candidates' leadership potential might be evaluated through examining these four categories.

Personal Attributes. This dimension undergirds the other three general dimensions, but ascertaining this information is no small task. In order to assess personal attributes, program planners must have a clear understanding of the individual qualities sought and how they are connected to the constructs of leadership and the objectives of the program. Guiding principles for the planning group include a focus on the characteristics of curiosity and daring and on information regarding experimentation and risk-taking behavior (e.g., how has the candidate dealt with adversity, success, and difficult challenges?).

Specific strategies for assessing strengths of candidates will be discussed in more detail as we look at particular role groups. In appraising these attributes, it is important to have substantive information. Conversations with significant people coupled with narrative accounts regarding personal attributes can be most helpful.

Professional Reputation. Certainly the candidate's professional reputation should be regarded as important. Characteristics of leadership that have bearing on professional reputation include trustworthiness and integrity. How successful has this candidate been in earning the trust of multiple constituencies and to what extent has he or she been an example to others?

Letters of reference serve as one source of information regarding this characteristic, but program planners would be well advised to extend this activity to include personal conversations with significant others with whom the candidate has been associated. This does not imply that letters of reference should be discounted. Rather, it implies that forms used for references may be misleading or skewed and rarely have provision for a thorough appraisal. Reference forms might include questions that elicit evidence—or lack thereof—of perseverance, compassion, and empathy. Once obtained, to what extent do the references agree about the candidate? It is incumbent on program planners to seek evidence from multiple sources.

Professional Experiences. This dimension includes an examination of employment history. The nature, duration, and locations of employment contribute to an assessment of the breadth and depth of the candidate's experience.

What criteria should be considered in equating professional experience with leadership characteristics? How can passion and a guiding vision be examined relative to professional experiences?

It is possible to discern the presence or absence of passion and vision by assessing the results of past professional leadership activities. Did candidates, for example, become organizationally involved beyond contractual obligations? Did they inspire commitment rather than rely on overt control? Did they challenge the status quo? Were they innovative? Were those with whom they worked challenged by their leadership?

Academic Preparation. This category relates to the candidate's record of academic achievement. One might examine such items as universities attended, transcripts of record, earned degrees, and areas of specialization. This examination can provide insight into the kind of student the candidate has been and his or her level of commitment as evidenced by degree completion. The reputation of the universities attended may help establish the quality of the candidate's preparation program. The areas of specialization provide information regarding the background and knowledge necessary to assume a particular position. Areas of specialization may be viewed in terms of the intensity of academic pursuits as well as the breadth of interests.

Certain academic requirements may be established by the university, the department, or the program planners. For example, minimum undergraduate and graduate grade-point averages, undergraduate and graduate majors and minors, and programs of studies can be considered if germane to the selection of participants in each of the role groups.

Developing the Selection Criteria

A preliminary matrix, as shown in Figure 2.2, may be used to examine the dimensions of personal attributes, professional reputation, professional experience, and academic preparation. Additional descriptors relative to specific contexts (e.g., characteristics deemed appropriate for administering in unique situations) may be added.

This effort by the internship staff, university faculty, district personnel, interns, and selected others may generate a comprehensive view of the types of individuals to be recruited and selected as well as procedures for selection. Candidate selection can be facilitated by using a matrix, such as that shown in Figure 2.3, that lists both the criteria and the sources of information about those qualities. Elements placed in this matrix may vary according to role, but several of the most important ones are described briefly below:

- *Innovativeness and creativity:* Generates and recognizes alternative solutions; receives and responds to others' ideas; demonstrates originality; effectively performs under pressure; responds to varied environments, tasks, responsibilities, and constituencies; tolerates ambiguity.
- *Educational values:* Has a clear personal philosophy; places priority on needs of students; is receptive to change and understands the need for stability; establishes goals and standards for self and others; maintains clear perspective of the role of school in society.

FIGURE 2.2: Role Groups, Recruitment, and Selection Criteria

	ROLE GROUPS			
SELECTION CRITERIA	Program Director	Site Administrators	Field Supervisors	Interns
Personal Attributes				
Professional Reputation				
Professional Experience				
Academic Preparation				

FIGURE 2.3: Selection Criteria and Data Sources

Selection Criteria	Data	Sources of Data
Innovativeness and Creativity		
Educational Values		
Group Leadership		
Human Relations		
Instructional Leadership and Supervison		
Communication		
Problem Analysis		
Administration of Curriculum		
Respect for Diversity		

- *Group leadership:* Senses and communicates vision; is self-confident; involves others; recognizes group needs and interacts effectively with groups; has a positive impact; performs consistently.
- *Human relations:* Perceives concerns; recognizes conflict; maintains confidentiality; is tactful and supportive regarding emotional issues.
- *Instructional leadership and supervision:* Understands and is well versed in instructional processes and techniques; evaluates relative to objectives and performance; employs good clinical supervision techniques.
- *Communication:* Is precise and concise in presenting facts and ideas; shares information readily and in a timely fashion; thinks of others' need-to-know requirements and interests; listens well.
- *Problem analysis:* Involves others in determining problem elements using relevant information; distinguishes problem significance; is adept in group processes and conflict resolutions; considers potential impact of alternative solutions; implements and evaluates solutions.

- *Administration of curriculum:* Relates to problems of inquiry, development, and evaluation; uses collaborative processes of deliberation; understands curriculum development at the philosophical and operational levels.
- *Respect for gender differences and ethnic diversity:* Acknowledges and respects varied ways of knowing and relating interpersonally; celebrates differences; promotes multiculturalism.

These areas are by no means exhaustive. Program planners are encouraged to incorporate additional criteria into the selection process.

EXERCISE 2.1
Role groups, selection, and recruitment criteria

The matrices shown in Figures 2.2 and 2.3 can be used as a stimulus for discussion by the parties involved in program design and implementation. The group can discuss what criteria for each of the four dimensions would be most essential in selecting candidates, given the nature of each of the four positions.

THE PROGRAM DIRECTOR

The program director is the one person on whose shoulders the entire program's reputation rests, whether warranted or not. Consequently, careful consideration must be given to this selection.

The recruitment and selection of the program director should focus on highly qualified individuals with significant and appropriate field experiences. The credibility of the program may hinge on the qualifications of the director. In the best of all worlds, and given the diversity of constituencies, the position should be filled with one who is a practitioner-scholar. Considerable time should be spent in developing appropriate criteria for the assessment of candidates for this position.

Selection Criteria

Personal Attributes.   Desirable personal attributes include the ability to work with groups formally as well as informally. Other qualities to look for include a high energy level, a sense of humor, active listening skills, and empathy for novices in learning situations. Knowledge of the principles of andragogy, and use of appropriate stategies in response to varied learning styles is significant. The ability to interact effectively with university and district personnel is of paramount importance.

Professional Reputation. Information from peers, colleagues, prior supervisors, and community members can provide valuable information about the professional reputation of candidates. It is advantageous to get written as well as oral feedback when feasible. Asking for feedback regarding specific criteria (checklists or open-ended questions) would assure more focused responses. It is imperative that the program director be highly respected by those with whom he or she will be in contact. The candidate must possess the qualities that make it likely that respect and a positive professional reputation can be earned.

Professional Experience. This involves an examination of both the *quantity* and *quality* of experiences, the roles/positions occupied, evidence of productivity, innovativeness, and knowledge of the geographic area. Adjunct faculty assignments at universities, continuing professional development, and first-hand experience of and knowledge regarding administrative internship programs are examples of such qualifications.

Initial information from application materials regarding professional experiences can guide further investigation. Subsequent interviews and checks can be guided by questions regarding leadership experiences such as: Have they been innovators and developers? Have they focused on people? Have they been their own person yet supported the organization? Have they demonstrated a long-range perspective?

Academic Preparation. Considerations might include such dimensions as the highest professional degree earned, quality of grades attained, recency of training, major areas of concentration, professional program content (e.g., an instructional-leadership as well as a management focus), and the quality of the institutions attended.

Examining the academic preparation relative to leadership can answer such questions as: Has the candidate completed what he or she has initiated? Are there indications of life-long learning? Has academic preparation helped the candidate gain knowledge and understanding about education in general and administration in particular?

Procedures for Recruitment and Selection

The use of professional organizations, national outlets, and professional publications (e.g., the *Chronicle of Higher Education*) can expand the pool from which applicants can be drawn. Great care and forethought must be taken in wording the notice. By doing so, the number of inquiries from those who do not meet requirements will be minimized and the challenges of the position will attract quality candidates.

Procedurally, the methods used for publicizing position openings must follow institutional, state, and federal guidelines. The following example of a position announcement for a program director indicates some particular qualities sought.

> The Department of Educational Administration seeks applications for the position of Director of its Administrative Internship Program. Minimum qualifications include advanced graduate work in educational administration; successful record as a principal (with preference given to candidates with some experience at different levels and at a district line position); and some familiarity with district administrative functions. Experience as an instructor at the university level is also highly desirable.
>
> Salary is negotiable, depending upon qualifications. Applications will be accepted until [date], with the appointment to begin [date]. Send vita, three letters of reference, and placement file to [address].

One of the best ways to attract applicants is through informal networking. Personal contacts may result in attracting applicants who otherwise would not give much consideration to the announcement. Informally "passing the word around" may yield a richer field of candidates from which to choose. A decision must be made about whether the search is to be national, regional, or local. This decision should be based on the type of position the program director will occupy (i.e., a full faculty line, lecturer, or adjunct status) and the fiscal arrangement for funding the position.

Inclusion of administrators from the field of educational administration, representatives from the university, and administrative interns in the screening and selection process provides some assurance that the director will have a viable support base.

Interviews may take many forms and may be either structured or semistructured. The interview committee should discuss expectations for the program director prior to agreement on interview procedures and be sure that these expectations are explored in the interview. Interviews might provide an opportunity for the candidates to discuss their visions for the program, ideas about leadership in educational administration, and philosophies of education in general. Alternatively, they might include questions related to the candidate's experiences, case study analysis, problem-solving activities, and knowledge of mentoring and adult learning.

Whichever interview procedures are selected, members of the interview committee should be representative of the constituencies to be served. The committee might include university and district personnel, program staff, former and current interns, and other interested parties having a stake in the program's success.

EXERCISE 2.2
Checklist for the assessment of candidates for program director

Using the criteria mentioned earlier, a checklist can be developed to evaluate each candidate. The checklist for the assessment of candidates for program director (Figure 2.4) can be used as a preliminary way to screen candidates before selecting finalists for interviews. Planning groups may use quantitative or qualitative indices or a combination of both. An index for professional experience may include a scale of factors to be multiplied by the number of years of service in education at each level:

5 points for service in line and staff positions
4 points for experience in varied staff positions
3 points for service in two staff positions
2 points for experience at one level of experience
1 point for service at the assistant level

The same type of scale can also be developed for the areas of personal attributes, professional reputation, and academic preparation.

FIELD SUPERVISORS

Field supervisors are responsible for serving as liaisons between the field and the university as well as between the site administrator and the intern. They are responsible for conducting site visits, documenting observations, advising, and maintaining open lines of communication with the interns, site administrators, and program director. Program designs may differ according to institution, but the role of those responsible for acting as liaisons between the university and the field is always vital.

Initial questions to be addressed by planners might include: What are the responsibilities of the field supervisors? What characteristics would enhance the fulfillment of these responsibilities? The qualities to consider include many of those listed in Figure 2.3. Beyond these, what specific considerations should be given to the dimensions of personal attributes, personal reputation, personal experience, and academic preparation?

Selection Criteria

Personal Attributes. Field supervisors must be capable of adept and responsive leadership. Depending on program design, these individuals may be the most visible members of the program staff at the district and school sites. They must be able to interact with each contact as astute representatives

FIGURE 2.4: Matrix for the Selection of Program Director

PERSONAL ATTRIBUTES			PROFESSIONAL REPUTATION		
Data	Data Sources		Data	Data Sources	
Scores			Scores		

PROFESSIONAL EXPERIENCES			ACADEMIC PREPARATION		
Data	Data Sources		Data	Data Sources	
Scores			Scores		

of the school district, program, and university. The field supervisors may serve as confidant(e)s for many constituencies. As such, they must be able to maintain confidences while suggesting alternatives.

Professional Reputation. The professional reputation of field supervisors rests largely with their ability to attain and maintain high levels of trust. The integrity of these individuals is critical. It is the field supervisors who are, for the most part, the liaisons between the intern, the site administrator, and the program staff. They must be team players, supportive colleagues, and viable mentors. Therefore candidates must show ample evidence of superior leadership performance as a former administrator.

Professional Experience. Experience in education—preferably in educational administration—is an important criterion. Generally, experience at the level at which interns are assigned is desirable. Program planners may also want to consider whether staff experience as well as line experience should be given attention.

Academic Preparation. Field supervisors should be academically prepared in education, with particular emphasis in educational administration. In addition, it is important to note whether there is evidence of continuing professional development.

One of the richest sources to be tapped for these positions is that of the growing group of retired administrators. Many of these individuals are knowledgeable about and familiar with local situations. The strength of this group is in-depth experience rather than recency of formal academic preparation. It is important, however, that they be able to interact with university faculty and be aware of current trends in the field of educational administration.

Procedures for Recruitment and Selection

Professional experience, professional reputation, and personal attributes are more important than formal academic preparation for this particular role. It is important to include representatives from multiple constituencies on the selection committee for field supervisors.

Figure 2.4, the matrix used for selection of a program director, may be used as well for the selection of candidates to be interviewed for this position. Each of these dimensions, as well as others, may have general as well as specific descriptors. It is suggested that multiple data sources be used to ensure rigorous examination. This data can then be scrutinized by the selection committee to screen for interviews and subsequent conversations.

SITE ADMINISTRATORS

Site administrators have a profound effect on the quality of interns' experiences. This much effort should go into identifying and choosing site administrators rather than accepting all comers. It should be viewed as a professional honor and an opportunity rather than an obligation.

Qualities for consideration may follow the criteria outlined in Figures 2.3 and 2.4. However, emphasis on particular dimensions may differ from that of other role players.

Selection Criteria

Personal Attributes. Personal attributes of site administrators include the ability to delegate responsibilities and serve as positive role models. It is important that program planners consider what traits are desirable in a role model prior to assessing those of individual candidates. For example, site administrators need to be able to listen actively and empathically to a wide range of individuals. Similarly, they must be willing to devote time to interns and to provide opportunities for growth while resisting using interns for mundane and unrelated tasks. This will facilitate successful experiences for both parties. Too often, interns have been used as glorified "go-fers."

Professional Reputation. The professional reputation of potential site administrators may be gleaned from those supervised, peers, and supervisors. It is important that perceptions come from multiple sources.

Assessment of professional reputation should focus on the level of esteem afforded site administrators in the professional community. Honors, awards, and recognition for professional accomplishments land credibility to positive subjective assessments. Attention to their levels of professional and community involvement can also provide substantive portraits of potential site administrators.

Site administrators must devote equal intensity and devotion to being good administrators (i.e., manage the enterprise) and good educators (i.e., provide instructional leadership). They must also have a global view rather than a territorial attitude or narrow perspective.

Professional Experience. Assessment of professional experiences focuses on the quality and quantity of administrative experiences. These experiences may include prior involvement with interns and other novice educators, coupled with personal experience in the area of the intern's aspiration. Extensive experience in the geographic area would also enhance the site administrator's ability to help interns acquire knowledge of the local cultural and political situation.

The ability to make explicit the reasons behind administrative actions is paramount. For many veteran administrators, such reasoning may have become unconscious. But reasons have to be retrieved at a conscious level for interns to be able to understand them, to be able to link cause with effect in observing and practicing administrative behavior.

Academic Preparation. Focus here might be on the recency of training and/or experiences, completion of a licensure program, evidence of continuing interaction with universities, and the rigor of preparation. These characteristics can be equated to those used in assessing candidates for field supervisors.

Information that reveals continuing professional development activities lends credence to the site administrator's commitment to learning and self-improvement, an important aspect of role modeling.

Procedures for Selection

The manner in which site administrators are selected depends, at least in part, on the design and structure of the internship program. Some programs require or permit interns to serve with administrators at schools where they maintain teaching positions, whereas others encourage interns to serve with administrators at an alternative, initially unfamiliar site. Interns who serve with administrators at their "home" site have advantages stemming from the presence of familiar colleagues as well as the knowledge of the administrator's leadership behavior and methods of operation. Interns who serve at alternate sites have no prior experience with the particular administrator but have the opportunity to develop a reputation with another administrator and constituencies. In short, the selection of site administrators involves consideration of many elements. Regardless of the structure of the program, the qualities listed in Figure 2.3 remain relatively constant.

If the future of education rests with those most able being placed in positions of leadership, it follows that those responsible for educating future educational leaders must be the most able. These selections and placements must be made with forethought and planning.

It is incumbent on the program director to attend district, regional, and statewide professional meetings to establish contacts and to disseminate program information. Potential site administrators may be asked to complete forms that elicit information regarding the qualities mentioned. This can be followed with personal communications and, if possible, interviews with administrators to enhance their understanding of the program and its inherent responsibilities.

Once an adequate number of interested respondents is accumulated and files are compiled, a selection committee may be appointed. The membership of this committee should include representative constituencies much like that for the selection of the director (i.e., it should include university and field-based personnel).

While a pool can be established in this manner, the final selections must take into account the match between intern characteristics and site administrator characteristics. This "chemistry" is the key to the parties' ability to work together in a mutually productive relationship. Since the leadership behavior and personal demeanor of the parties affects the quality of this relationship, attention must be given to this "fit." Diversity may provide richness, but particular characteristics may have an adverse effect on the experience for both parties.

ADMINISTRATIVE INTERNS

The recruitment and selection of interns is important because the future of educational leadership rests with these individuals. What procedures can be developed to assure that excellent candidates are recruited and selected? What characteristics are most worthy of examination? How do these relate to the potential for leadership?

Selection Criteria

Personal Qualities.   Personal qualities sought in administrative interns must include confidence, ability to work with multiple constituencies, tolerance for ambiguity, high energy level, and willingness to devote time to endeavors. Examining attributes for successful leadership might include exploring such dimensions as communication skills, philosophical assumptions, and work ethic. This analysis may take varied approaches, depending on the structure and intensity of the assessment process.

Particular descriptors might include those found in Figure 2.5, which examines leadership attributes and management skills. High-performing candidates would likely have demonstrated potential for leadership by engaging in prior leadership responsibilities at the school level and exhibiting positive characteristics in their behaviors.

Professional Reputation.   Recommendations from supervisors attesting to prior involvement, successes, and potential as an administrator portray

FIGURE 2.5:   Leadership Attributes and Management Skills

LEADERSHIP ATTRIBUTES	MANAGEMENT SKILLS
Motivation	Communication
Ambition	Organization
Creativity	Management of Time
Risk-Taking	Coordination and Scheduling
Tolerance of Stress	Insuring Effectiveness of Strategies
Self-Evaluation	Diagnosing
Tenacity	Supervising
Empathy	
Articulateness	

professional reputation. It is important that interns be proactively recruited by educational leaders.

Professional Experience.   While state licensure requirements vary, candidates should have at least three years of successful teaching experience in order to be familiar with the organization. Volunteer work in administrative areas gives some indication of interest and capabilities, and data regarding effectiveness in this work should be examined. It is a key aspect to examine.

Academic Preparation.   Academic preparation must provide some assurance that a knowledge base has been established prior to fieldwork. Enrollment in a graduate program in educational administration before entering an internship program is one way of demonstrating this. Indicators of success as a student might include grade-point averages and entrance-exam scores. Research by Martin and Kelly (1989) suggests that undergraduate grade-point average is an effective screening device, since it is correlated with eight performance inventory skill areas and scores on National Teacher Examination tests. It is also important to examine the candidates' preparation in one or more curricular areas, which provides some evidence of breadth of knowledge and interest. Given the emphasis being placed on instructional leadership, interns should have content-area emphasis as well as some background in administration.

A writing sample on a subject chosen by the applicant or selected by program staff may attest to a candidate's ability to communicate effectively. The writing sample shows both the depth of knowledge on a particular subject and the ability to analyze and synthesize information. Additionally, a topic chosen by the applicant provides insight into what the candidate perceives as an important issue.

Procedures for Recruitment and Selection

Recruitment of interns can be thought of a as a three-step process:

1. Identifying the potential intern
2. Making direct contact with students during the application phase
3. Conducting an initial screening

Internships required by academic departments and state licensing agencies create a natural flow of students into programs. Program planners need to pay particular attention to *proactive recruitment* of potential interns rather than waiting for self-selected candidates to apply. Active recruitment measures enhance the likelihood that those who apply and are selected will be the most able candidates. District personnel, site administrators, and educational administration students (or intern alumni) should be contacted and encouraged to identify potential candidates.

There are a number of ways that the availability of programs can be advertised. How this is done is largely dependent on the goals of the program and district policies. Initially, information regarding the program must be made available to personnel in cooperating districts. This is best done through a personal approach; that is, visiting with district personnel. Once the districts have been apprised of program purposes, brochures that describe the program, including timelines and procedures for application, can then be distributed to faculty and staff at school sites. The program staff can also distribute this information at a regularly scheduled administrators' meeting, at which time, they can also present an overview of the program and entertain questions.

When the names of interested applicants are made available, it is advantageous for the program staff to make direct contact with potential interns to make information available to them and ascertain their areas of interest. Information such as academic background, professional employment experiences, and aspirations should be obtained at this time. Candidates may be asked to furnish documentation regarding academic information, letters of intent, and letters of support from site administrators. Additional data might include a brief paper setting forth their educational platform/philosophy.

Once the candidate has been admitted to the graduate school and the department, procedures for screening candidates into the internship program may begin. We strongly encourage this two-step process because it allows the program staff to review information on academic and work backgrounds, career goals, rationale for interest, and ability to undertake the internship. It allows the staff to assess whether the student's goals and potential as a leader are consonant with program goals. This activity may be used for out-counseling, for identification of individual program priorities and growth plans, and to identify potential placements for students.

It is advisable to have interns examine the inventory for the assessment of readiness for job placement in Figure 6.1. It is best to review these items early in the program so that appropriate measures may be taken for their fulfillment. In addition, the completion of a survey on perceived or anticipated experiences may also assist in both planning and evaluation efforts. Sample questions for this survey are given in Figure 6.2. These questions may be rephrased upon completion of the program and utilized as a comparative (pre- and post-) aspect of evaluation.

Figure 2.6, which takes into consideration personal attributes, personal reputation, professional experience, and academic preparation, can be used for screening the pool of applicants. Much of this information can be obtained from department or college application materials.

After a review of the initial application materials (transcripts, letters of reference, letters of intent, and survey questions), selections may be made for candidates to participate in an assessment center process. This can be one of the best ways to acquire a subjective understanding of prospective interns. This process may be modeled after one or a combination of established pro-

FIGURE 2.6: Matrix for the Assessment of Intern Applicants

	Personal Attributes	Professional Reputation	Professional Experience	Academic Preparation
Name	Data/Source	Data/Source	Data/Source	Data/Source

FIGURE 2.7: Assessment Center Activity Score Sheet

Name: _____ Phone: (H) _____

Address: (H) _____ (W) _____

     (W) _____

     _____

ASSESSMENT CENTER ACTIVITIES:

	Score Tally
1. Interview score . . . . Comments:	_____
2. In-basket score . . . . Comments:	_____
3. Presentation score . . . . Comments:	_____
4. Writing exercise score . . . . Comments:	_____
5. Group activities score . . . . Comments:	_____
6. Other	_____

Action Taken _____ Accepted   TOTAL SCORE _____
              _____ Not Accepted

cesses such as that of the National Association of Secondary School Principals (see Milstein & Feidler, 1989). As a final phase in the selection process, this can provide additional data about the candidates. As an example, a group problem-solving activity can yield data on how candidates function and what roles they play in a group setting. Individual presentations may provide information on candidates' ability to communicate about an area or project of interest. Interns' presence and demeanor can be assessed through an interview process. An example of selection information and assessment center activity data is shown in Figure 2.7. (Assessment centers are described in more detail in Chapter 3.)

Once all information is collated, a representative committee of internship program staff, district personnel, and university faculty can collaborate in the final selection of interns.

IN CONCLUSION

It is increasingly important to examine the way in which individuals who will lead our schools—and those who prepare them to lead our schools—are selected. The quality of our schools, which rests on the ability of their future administrators, is the central concern in selecting and recruiting internship program directors, field supervisors, site administrators, and administrative interns. It is through the concentrated effort of school districts and universities that the selection, preparation, and licensing of talented and dynamic leaders will be accomplished.

CHAPTER 3

Designing the Internship Program

IN DESIGNING an internship program, consideration must be given to patterns of responsibility and authority. Responsibility for internship programs can be the sole domain of a university or a school system, or it can be shared cooperatively between a university and one or more school systems. It is also possible to develop two or more responsibility patterns to meet different needs if this is warranted. A decision must be made about which arrangement is most appropriate and where ultimate responsibility lies prior to contemplating other elements of the design.

PATTERNS OF RESPONSIBILITY AND AUTHORITY

Universities and Internship Programs

The most common approach is for internships to be offered by universities. This option is most appropriate if there are many school districts to be served and it is difficult to develop and maintain cooperative responsibilities. Positive aspects of this approach include minimal coordination requirements and increased potential for timely responses to intern needs. This option may also garner a higher degree of faculty support because it allows faculty to retain control of and responsibility for the academic program and internship activities. The shortcomings of this arrangement are that universities working in isolation can easily become out of touch with the needs and priorities of school systems and, just as easily, can neglect to develop the networks of relationships required to identify good internship sites and subsequent placement possibilities.

School Districts and Internship Programs

Large school systems may decide to develop their own internship programs for aspiring administrators. They may do so to assure a continuing human resource base for their leadership positions, especially if local institutions of higher education do not seem to be responsive to their needs or if no university-based programs exist in the immediate geographic area.

The advantages of a school district–based program are the likelihood that the system's priorities will be emphasized and that system leaders will focus considerable attention on internship activities. Weaknesses include the danger that the program, although rich in field experiences, will be deficient in those elements that a university may be best suited to offer—reflection and academic content. Further, it is possible that internship programs, as only one of many projects directed by central office role players, will become lost in the shuffle.

School District/University Cooperative Programs

There is a symbiotic relationship between universities and school systems that can be capitalized on through shared responsibility for an internship program. Potential candidates come from school districts, generally as teachers, and intend to return to those districts as administrators. School districts, therefore, have a stake in the initial identification and subsequent preparation of candidates. They also have an intimate knowledge of suitable sites and outstanding site administrators. However, school systems are unlikely to have the time or resources to provide the knowledge base to the extent required. Universities have the ability to provide this knowledge and the potential to provide supervision of the program. They must, however, depend on school systems for the availability of sites and daily supervision of interns.

The difficulty with a cooperative approach is that it requires much coordination between organizations. Aside from the time required for coordination, it also means that a university and one or more school systems must convince several policy-making bodies that it is appropriate to develop interorganizational mechanisms that facilitate the development and maintenance of the program.

Multiple Responsibility Patterns for Programs

Some situations might warrant the development of alternative responsibility patterns. For example, a university may be pressed to prepare administrators for school systems in a large metropolitan area as well as for many smaller rural systems throughout the state. Cooperative responsibility might be feasible between the university and the larger, more geographically proximate systems, while the realities of working with distant rural systems might require the university to retain sole responsibility for field-based training. In such cases, it may be appropriate to develop and maintain two programs with different responsibility patterns (e.g., a cooperative responsibility pattern might be best for the metropolitan area and sole university responsibility for the rural situations).

Selecting a Pattern

There is no one right answer to the question of which responsibility pattern is best. Each approach, as noted, has advantages and disadvantages. Further, particular situations must be taken into consideration. Those involved in decision making regarding patterns of responsibility may benefit from in-depth discussion concerning such questions as:

1. What is the history of administrative preparation in the area? Has the university tended to operate in splendid isolation? Or is there a history of cooperation that can form a solid base for shared responsibility?
2. What are the demographics? How many school systems are, or could be, involved? How large are they? How geographically dispersed are they?
3. How open are the organizations to the possibility of shared responsibility at this time?

The examination of questions such as these can yield information which affects the planning of key elements in program design.

This approach concentrates on internship programs in which the university serves as the key party in the responsibility pattern, with as much focus on partnerships as possible. If readers' situations call for conceptualizing different control patterns, the ideas presented here will need to be adapted accordingly.

KEY ELEMENTS IN PROGRAM DESIGN

This section deals with major considerations that program designers should explore in formulating the key elements of an internship program. These include critical logistic considerations, program sequence, planning of and participants in the design and conduct of the program, and promoting the program to multiple constituencies.

Critical Logistic Considerations

Many issues regarding logistics are often overlooked in initial program planning stages. Consideration should be given to such logistics as the options and benefits of alternative financial arrangements, clock hours to be

portunity to experience different leadership behaviors and school cultures.
t the intern also must become accepted by persons at the site—and the
gree to which the intern becomes involved hinges on the degree of this
:eptance.

Resolving these issues means putting aside excuses and notions of "ac-
)ted" or "traditional" ways of doing things. It requires forethought, crea-
ity, and risk taking on the part of program planners.

gram Sequence

Prior to beginning the planning, representatives of key groups—stu-
nts, faculty, and school district leaders—need to consider some basic for-
t questions regarding the program. How will the program flow? How will
idemic coursework and field experiences be coordinated? Milstein (1990)
tes at least four different approaches that might be considered:

The linear approach. This rather traditional approach is one in which
campus-based learnings are pursued first and clinical experiences comprise
the culminating program experiences. The assumption is that students
must first master a knowledge base before they can maximize their learning
in the field.

The dialectic approach. This approach assumes that learning takes place best
when it combines acquisition of a knowledge base with application in real-
world settings. Internship programs based on this assumption involve students in field experiences at the same time they take campus-based seminars.

The reflective practice approach. This approach is based on the belief that
theory is best learned if it is based on experience. This implies that practice
must come early and that theory building becomes a possibility only as
students gain an experiential foundation.

The developmental approach. This approach assumes the need for a foundation of knowledge and theory but also assumes that field experiences must
begin early in the program so that these theories can be tested in practice.
The implication is that campus-based activities will initially be the primary
focus but that, over time, there will be an increasing level of field-based
activities and a comparable reduction of academic seminar activities.

There is no evidence that any one approach is superior, although there is
reasing criticism of the linear approach and more support for one form or
other of blending knowledge acquisition with practice. Past experiences
d preferences of university faculty, school system leaders, and internship
rticipants must be taken into consideration in deciding which approach or
nbination of approaches to pursue. What is important is that alternatives

required of interns at their particular sites, placement of inter
other sites, and assignment of program staff to full- or part-ti

Financial Arrangements. Program financial arrangem
those funded as full-time sabbaticals to those in which intern
time positions while completing academic coursework and fi
The benefit of and intern's being fully immersed in an admin
ship is obvious—but this is often a financial impossibility. Cor
who maintain full-time positions while involved in academic c
field experiences are often insufficiently involved in the full r
istrative realities. Therefore, it is incumbent on program de
innovative in their approach to financial/fiscal arrangements
involved, as well as the programs, remain solvent.

One possibility is to provide interns with stipends and
through fellowships. A variety of innovative strategies are ava
be developed to fund the program.

The approach taken should be the one that is most finar
geous to all parties while maintaining a credible and effective
perience. Those responsible for funding arrangements must e>
ing avenues and be open to creative alternatives.

Time in the Field. The time required for the intern to
varies. Many states require a minimum number of clock hou
experience for licensure purposes, while others relegate these d
universities. Coupled with this is the issue of the benefits and
of one semester as opposed to two, and days per week as opp
per day.

An intern who is involved in a year-long, or two-semestei
the advantage of a more extended vantage point. The one-sem
does not allow the intern involvement in such time-bound sit
opening of a school compared with the closing of a school. Sim
per day does not enable interns to gain a true administrative
as great a depth as would, perhaps, a day per week. Each of
however, has limitations. Again, it is important to balance co
to achieve the greatest good for the intern, the program, and
encies served.

Home or Alternate Sites. The question of intern placeme
alternate sites must also be considered early in program plannii
at the home site gives an intern the advantage of familiarity wi
the potential disadvantage is that these colleagues will perceive
his or her "old" role. Placement at an alternate site affords

be considered and that an approach be agreed upon by all involved parties before a program is designed in detail.

Planning the Design and Conduct of the Program

It is essential to involve key people when designing the program, both to obtain commitment to the program and to ensure that ideas and plans are generated. The participation of student/interns, school district personnel, and university faculty is crucial when planning short- and long-range strategies.

In the initial planning of any new program, representatives must interact as a group to define the purposes of the internship program. The next key step is to design the operational procedures that will contribute to meeting the purposes. Key players need time to discuss their philosophies about what should occur in an internship program, build consensus about program expectations, and ensure the preparation of outstanding administrators. This contributes to building a foundation for communication on which to develop goals, objectives, and activities. It may also serve to facilitate discussion on how program expectations can be provided and the roles of the university and the school district.

Using any one specific planning model is not as important as answering key questions about how the program will be implemented, by whom, for whom, with what resources, and in what time frame.

EXERCISE 3.1
The planning process

Early in the process of designing the internship program, a thoughtful discussion of planning issues should be undertaken. Some questions, as suggested by Cunningham & Nystrand's (1969) planning model, include:

1. Where are we?
2. Where do we want to go?
3. What resources will we commit to get there?
4. How do we get there?
5. When will it be done?
6. Who will be responsible?
7. What will be the impact on human resources?
8. What data will be needed to measure progress?

This discussion may be framed around the general categories shown in Figure 3.1. Objectives should be stated clearly and result from consensus. This figure may be used to provide an overview of the objectives; their rela-

FIGURE 3.1: Matrix for Use as a Planning Model

Objectives	Status at present	Resources	Procedures	Completion dates	Responsibility/ authority	Evaluation

tive status at the present time; availability of and need for resources (human, fiscal, material) necessary to reach the objectives; procedures for attaining objectives; targeted completion dates; responsibility and/or authority patterns for reaching objectives; and methods for evaluating attainment of objectives.

Participation in the Design and Conduct of the Program

The importance of including key players in the planning process has already been noted. The conclusions reached by these participants are a crucial element in that process.

Student/Interns and Alumni. These members can be an invaluable resource in the planning and design process. They are in a strong position to identify strengths and needs of the program. They also have an immediate and critically important stake in the process. Their involvement can also contribute to their own learning about the planning process in a context that has potential short- and long-range significance. The formation of networks among participants, as well as cohort development among interns, may also be promoted. Mentoring relationships may also be initiated during this process. Students can learn the steps involved in the planning process as well as varied models for using long- and short-range procedures. Involvement in this process can help interns work through problems and plan strategies as administrators.

School District Personnel. Since school districts will ultimately be the employing agencies, their input is essential. Through internships, districts can not only identify candidates for potential job openings but also provide them with the experience needed to grow into successful administrators. School districts reap the benefits when administrators who join their systems can solve problems, share leadership, offer new ideas and perspectives, and relate current research and theory.

In addition to recruitment of future leaders, internships give school districts an opportunity to recognize and further develop the leadership skills of interns by placing them with site administrators who can provide positive role modeling. Clearly, an important aspect of the site administrator–intern relationship is for site administrators to demonstrate to interns the various aspects of the position. In this sense, they are "grooming-mentoring" students for roles as administrators (Swoboda & Miller, 1986). The selection of successful leaders as site administrators and the degree of intern involvement in district functions are vital to establishing a collegial network and professional reputation.

Representatives from school districts are in the best position to know what districtwide activities can complement and otherwise expand on the professional development of interns. Their input might include such information as what districtwide activities could be made available to administrative interns (e.g., workshops for new administrators, meetings, negotiations, budget preparation sessions, staff development sessions, and staff evaluation). It is imperative that the interns' experiences include as many administrative situations and responsibilities as time and opportunity permit. This includes attending, observing, and participating in meetings, conferences, and staff development activities in settings outside as well as at the school site. For this to occur, the partners in planning the design and implementation of the program should consider these issues in the initial planning.

To the extent that school district leaders participate in planning, interns will have increased site-based opportunities to demonstrate mastery of those skills and areas of expertise required of an educational administrator.

Educational Administration Faculty Members. Faculty department members play an important part in the planning process. In order to develop and maintain a cohesive and collaborative partnership, university faculty must understand the purposes, design, and conduct of an internship program. A common criticism about many internship programs is that educational administration faculty members play little if any meaningful role in the effort. The stereotypical view of internship programs is that they are either passed around among reluctant (usually junior) faculty members or that a practitioner is employed to conduct the program, thus relieving the faculty of the "burden."

If the internship program is to be viewed as an integral part of the overall preparation program, the attitudes and behaviors of faculty in many universities must change. The probability of constructing a more focused and co-ordinated internship program is dependent on this change.

It is possible to create enthusiasm and involvement on the part of the faculty, but only through sustained effort. Several steps must be taken. The department chairperson, or equivalent, must strongly sponsor the program if it is to gain initial acceptance. Firm leadership on the part of the chairperson is necessary to offset initial resistance, which can arise from such factors as fear of inadequacy in advising field efforts, reluctance to upset routines, and concern about being diverted from interests of higher priority. The chairperson must be an advocate, a resource person, and an effective institutional politician.

Faculty members might be given workload credit for advising interns. If the program is successful, such advisory duties will take up significant portions of the faculty members' time. Giving workload credit can send a clear message to faculty members, especially those who may initially be resistant. The program director can assist in this process by helping faculty members define their roles. This includes clarifying what is expected regarding supervision, discussing activities and objectives interns will be pursuing, and promoting the reflective evaluation of the experience through formative and summative analysis. The program director can facilitate this by bringing together members of the team—the intern, site administrator, field supervisors, and faculty advisor—to explore goals, activities, and procedures.

Ultimately, the project director is the key link in the entire process. The director is the orchestrator of the effort and is in the best position to know whether faculty members are confident and enthusiastic. When such is not the case, it is incumbent upon the director to discuss problems with those involved in order to rectify them.

The directorship should be a full-time position in order to permit this kind of interaction and involvement. Part-time status does not allow the time necessary to create and sustain the quality of programs. When a full-time director is in charge, many of the problems that plague programs with part-time directors are alleviated.

A collective design effort that includes students, school district leaders, and university faculty will result in a program for which each feels responsibility and ownership—two prime factors in program success.

Promoting the Program to Multiple Constituencies

Publicizing the internship program is critical in maximizing school district sponsorship and in attracting outstanding candidates. Responsibilities for promoting the program can be shared by local school districts and the university to ensure that all teachers and other personnel receive information about the program. Promotion can be accomplished through a variety of strategies.

Contact by Principals. One of the most meaningful promotional activities is personal contact by principals with outstanding employees at their particular sites. Thus the program director should meet with principals and ask them to encourage prospective administrators to apply to the program. In addition, the director should make presentations at district meetings and ask that articles about the program be placed in district publications.

Open Meetings. Another way of promoting the program is to conduct meetings for interested candidates. At such meetings, it is important to have representation from the university faculty, school district administration and, perhaps, program alumni to discuss purposes and benefits of the program. When superintendents, assistant superintendents, principals, and other administrators participate in such meetings, their presence and contributions lend credibility and prestige to the program. Participating administrators and current interns can be asked to endorse the program and describe it in greater detail than is possible in a brochure or other materials. Such a meeting provides excellent opportunities to answer questions from those interested in participating in the internship program. Through this avenue, prospective candidates are given adequate information and a chance to reconsider and evaluate initial interests and motivations.

Graduate Seminars.   At the university level, it is important for faculty members to have an understanding of the program so that they can serve as resources for their advisees and other students concerning the program. Many graduate courses are comprised of part-time students who would otherwise be uninformed about such programs. Faculty members can distribute materials about the program to these students.

Brochures.   Written information in the form of brochures is also important. Procedures for developing program brochures will vary with institutions. As in the design stage, it would be useful for the program director, university faculty, and school district representatives to develop a draft cooperatively. Alumni and current interns can provide valuable suggestions regarding the contents of the brochure.

Elements for consideration in developing a program brochure might include:

Program purpose
Criteria for participation
Description of supervision procedures
Description of field experiences
Description of the academic course of study
Information on funding and stipends
Instructions and deadlines for application and admittance

DESIGNING THE INTERN SELECTION PROCESS

Practitioners and scholars alike believe that the quality of leadership of our educational organizations is directly related to organizational effectiveness. Thus we need to carefully review how prospective leaders are selected. Given that the quality of interns recruited and selected serves as the barometer for program success, how can the selection process be positively influenced by using university faculty, school district personnel, and community expertise? The following section presents a brief overview of traditional processes and suggested alternative approaches for the selection of interns.

Traditional Processes

Traditional selection processes include such things as letters of reference, interviews, academic records, and writing samples. Such documents provide information about the character of the individual as perceived by self and others. Much insight can be gained from reviewing these documents with respect to the candidates' aptitudes and abilities. However, these may not be sufficient as a basis for making the best selections because data gathered through these conventional means are often of questionable value. For example, letters of reference may be hard to evaluate, especially if they come from sources with whom those making decisions are unfamiliar. In addition, reference letters are often incomplete or inaccurate (McCleary & Ogawa, 1985). For example, supervisors who make recommendations may be guided by biased and incomplete personal impressions of subordinates (Baltzell & Dentler, 1983). Similarly, interviews often fail to garner comparable information from all candidates.

Utilizing Assessment Centers

Improved candidate selection is enhanced when additional in-depth, behaviorally anchored information can be gathered on potential leaders. Such is the case with assessment centers, where performance in simulated situations can become a basis for examining behavior in actual settings. Gathering data through assessment centers as well as through traditional means enhances the ability to assess key leadership behaviors and, hence, the ability to select the best candidates.

The assessment center can provide a good beginning for the socialization process. If the assessment center process is guided by key personnel from the university and participating school districts, a dialogue ensues as objectives are planned and implemented. Staff members have an opportunity to review data and performance records, discuss strengths and weaknesses, and rate each candidate. Such dialogue with other assessors and observers can also enhance participants' commitment to the internship program and to the interns selected to participate.

The assessment center approach allows for increased objectivity. As described by Milstein and Bobroff (1988), the assessment center can develop objective data on candidates that aid in making selections on the basis of merit. Discussions can be much more objective and comprehensive than they would be without the assessment center data. Decision makers have a much more realistic view of the applicants and thus better information on which to build preliminary recommendations.

The assessment center process varies, but it often includes:

- *Presentations:* Each candidate explains a contribution he or she has made to the field of education.
- *Group activities:* These involve problem-solving exercises in a small-group setting (e.g., building a paper tower in a group), followed by debriefing during which the behavior of group members is analyzed in terms of its relation to the group process and to leadership; the exercise concludes with a discussion of how the lessons learned in the activity can be applied in a school leadership situation.
- *In-basket activities and case-study responses:* Here candidates respond to examples of situations that they might encounter in an administrative position.
- *Individual interviews:* Here questions are, for the most part, broad and open ended.
- *Writing exercises:* Here candidates demonstrate their critical thinking and problem-solving skills in responding to a variety of issues.

Assessors might include practitioners, university faculty, current administrative interns, and business and community leaders. Preparation might include prior readings about assessment centers and a planning session before the event to familiarize participants with the nature and purpose of each activity and procedures for observing and evaluating.

The assessment center could be used by school districts and departments of educational administration with minimal expense. With simplicity in design and through advanced preparation, assessor training can be minimal. The time the director and secretary spend preparing materials to be used, and perhaps arranging refreshments for participants who donate their services, should also be minimal.

DESIGNING INTERN CLINICAL ACTIVITIES

Intern activities occur at two primary locations—in field settings and on campus. In both settings careful planning will maximize the benefit that interns gain from the clinical activities.

Activities in Field Settings

The field (i.e., the school site or its equivalent) is where interns learn how site administrators manage and lead. There is no substitute for this experience of administrative dynamics; only such real-world involvement can give interns the experiential base by which to measure their growth and development as administrators.

Administrators' activities are of two very different sorts: (1) They must tend to the daily management of the enterprise, but (2) they must also be concerned with planning and change (i.e., the leadership of the enterprise). Therefore field-based clinical activities should encompass both managerial and leadership functions. Interns must experience both dimensions to develop an understanding of the importance of both.

Management Activities.   Management activities are those that focus on the maintenance of routines. These activities must be accomplished if teachers and students are to be able to fulfill their responsibilities. It is important that interns have sufficient opportunities to observe and, as appropriate, be involved in management activities. We can view these administrative activities according to *competency areas,* or to the *sequential and cyclical school activities.*

Professional associations and state departments of education (see lists in Appendix B) have devised standards by which to assess administrators' competence in particular aspects of their role. Management activities should concentrate on the competency areas of instructional leadership, communications, management of school climate, management of resources, and policy awareness, all of which are crucial to an administrative intern's professional development. It is suggested that interns and site administrators "microplan" specific intern tasks for each of these competency areas. The matrix in Figure 3.2 may be used as a framework for this activity.

Activities should differentiate between those that interns will be expected to observe and those that they will be expected to participate in or conduct from the beginning of the internship to its completion. A typical, but by no means exhaustive, list of such activities might include the following:

Opening of school activities
   Assignment of students to teachers
   Placement of teachers in grade levels and subjects
   Student registration
   Preparation of personnel manuals
   Preparation of duty schedules

FIGURE 3.2: Matrix for Planning Intern Activities

Competency Areas	Activities	Evaluation: How, who, when?
Instructional leadership		
Communications		
Management of school climate		
Management of resources		
Policy Awareness		

Interviewing new staff members
Preparation of the budget
Planning for information dissemination to faculty, students, and parents
Faculty observation, supervision and evaluation
Staff development
Involvement in school attendance and discipline programs
School climate surveys
Master schedules
Program evaluation
Parent/student/community relations programs
Extracurricular activities
Textbook and materials ordering
Administrative and faculty meetings
District, state, and national meetings

Interns, site administrators, and field supervisors should compile a comprehensive list of daily management activities that are conducted by administrators over the course of a year. This exercise can serve all parties as they plan for intern observations and participation at the site.

Leadership Activities. Clinical programs should also provide interns with many opportunities to be involved in leadership activities. Being competent in the management of daily routines is necessary but not sufficient.

Effective administrators need to be adept at such leadership activities as goal setting, strategic planning, and problem solving. Society is marked by change and, as such, administrators must be willing and able to engage in activities that go beyond technical management concerns.

Interns should undertake a long-term problem-solving project to assure that leadership is emphasized (See Appendix A). The project area can be determined in consultation with site administrators and field supervisors or identified through needs assessment. Whatever project is selected, interns should have projects that require clarification, planning, development of alternative solutions, implementation, and evaluation of outcomes. The project should be related to one or more of the competency areas, and the intern should be responsible for all of its stages. Examples of possible project areas include school improvement, community relations, student programs, incentive programs for faculty, school-community-business liaisons, or communication.

Finally, interns should be expected to maintain a *log*, or *journal*, of their experiences in the field. The journal can facilitate structured ways of looking at daily experiences. The journal might include introspection regarding such questions as: What situations occurred? What decisions were made? Why were they made as they were? What could have been done differently? What learnings were acquired?

Keeping a journal can be an invaluable tool that enables the intern to identify patterns of thought and behavior over time. It can also be used for discussion and analysis among the intern, site administrators, and field supervisors. Further, it can serve as a stimulus for discussions at internship seminars.

Journals are not something with which many interns will have had prior experience or feel competent and comfortable in keeping at the outset. The skills involved in keeping a journal (e.g., using ethnographic approaches, avoiding judgments in favor of recording behaviorally anchored information) should be discussed in some depth. Inviting someone to a seminar session who is adept at journal keeping can provide helpful direction.

On-Campus Experiences

Although the major focal point of the intern's activities are field-based, there are supportive activities that can and should be conducted at the university or other sites. The site situation provides opportunity for direct observation and involvement in administrative activities, but it does not ensure that interns will be able to abstract the full measure of meaning (e.g., relationships, patterns, and directions) from these activities.

What is required is a complementary set of experiences that enrich the interns' ability to synthesize learnings and deepen perceptions regarding the role of administration. In other words, the internship experience must be more than "on-the-job" training.

While each internship program requires unique elements in the design of activities appropriate to particular situations, there is a clear agenda of activities that could be incorporated into most programs.

Sorting through Field-Based Phenomena. A university-based internship seminar can be a valuable forum where interns share observations and experiences. The program staff can guide discussion so that interns are able to process events occurring at the site.

This effort is both *reactive* and *proactive*. It is reactive in that it legitimizes aspects of administrative phenomena that require discussion and clarification. It is proactive in that the program staff can examine issues (e.g., leadership approaches, conflict management, motivational strategies) and elicit site-based examples to provide the basis for discussion. The more these issues are shared by participants, the greater the likelihood that interns will maximize learnings.

Skill Development. Adults learn best when they see immediate results from their efforts. In the case of the internship, reality testing creates the desire to learn ways of improving skills. For example, if communication does not seem clear, ways of improving this skill can be explored. Similarly, if efforts to motivate faculty are not effective, an examination of alternative motivational strategies can be undertaken. The internship seminar offers excellent opportunities to focus on skill development. A willingness to take risks and the ability of the program staff to teach skills is required.

Clarification of Leadership Styles. For many interns, site-based experiences provide the first opportunity to play a meaningful leadership role with other adults in a work environment. During this formative period they can benefit from exploring their own leadership styles. Within the framework of the internship seminar, as well as in other campus-based settings, interns can benefit from taking leadership style inventories and receiving constructive feedback.

Professional Development Opportunities. These activities can support interns' growth if they are planned as a set of interrelated learning opportunities. They should be conceptualized as growth activities that can be engaged in locally, regionally, and nationally. Interns can gain new perspectives about professional development that enrich and encourage life-long learning habits by clarifying objectives and searching out professional opportunities to enhance these objectives. Information regarding professional associations involved in the professional development of educational administrators may be found in Appendix B.

Clarification and Expansion of Values and Beliefs. As a result of the intern's field-based experiences and related activities, a platform of beliefs and values will begin to take shape. This platform should be challenged and honed at this formative stage of development. As potential administrators, interns need to understand and further develop their values.

Cohort Development. The internship, and subsequent career moves into administration, can be enhanced by purposeful development of a cohort. The support groups that are developed during this challenging activity are quite important. They go beyond the "misery loves company" syndrome to provide peer-group support, clarification of ideas and perceptions, career opportunities, and professional relations long after the internship is concluded. For these reasons, the internship staff should encourage cohort development through social activities, simulations, role playing, and other exercises as well as reflections on field experiences.

Learning about the System and Networking. To be an effective school leader, administrators must have a good sense of how the larger system functions and how it can be accessed. Given this, interns should have opportunities to learn how the elements of school systems operate and interrelate and to become aware of those who direct the functions.

Much of this can be accomplished by having key school district leaders share perceptions of their roles and the roles of other administrators. Formally arranged visits to district-level offices can also be beneficial in this regard.

In addition to gaining skills and confidence in their potential as administrators, interns need to become familiar with local and state educational decision makers. "Who you know" is critically important for gaining access, creating networks, and expanding an administrator's ability to influence. Networking is discussed more fully in Chapter 6.

Completion of Licensure/Certification Requirements. Licensure or certification typically requires completion of a minimum number of hours in specific areas, as well as the expectation of an internship or equivalent field experience. These requirements can be attended to during the course of the internship. For this to occur, required course offerings must be coordinated by university faculty. The earlier that these plans are formulated, the greater the likelihood that they will be met with minimal disruption.

EVALUATION

Evaluation is the focus of Chapter 7. The purpose of noting it here is to encourage program designers to anticipate this activity when designing the clinical program. Much of the data required for an evaluation can be collected during and after the internship. However, this can happen only if it is planned and built into the program design.

Evaluation should be thought of as both formative and summative. Formative evaluation requires gathering data both before the program begins and while it is in progress. Whether these data are attitudinal or behavioral, qualitative or quantitative, the purpose is to establish benchmarks against which growth and change may be measured.

Evaluations should be conducted to assess interns' progress and the program's adequacy. Evaluation of interns requires gathering data that indicate levels of growth and change as well as areas for further focus. Evaluation of the program is intended to ensure a continuation of its strengths and a modification of its weaknesses. In our changing world, a program can easily become obsolete if it is not regularly monitored. Various sample evaluation questionnaires are included in Appendix C.

IN CONCLUSION

Program staff, administrators, and students are encouraged to work collaboratively in the planning and implementation of clinical efforts. This process is as important as the product. Establishing a sense of "ownership" among participants greatly influences the accomplishment of purposes and objectives.

CHAPTER 4

The Knowledge Base of the
Internship Program

THE KNOWLEDGE BASE in administrative preparation has long been a topic of debate. The education and training of school administrators has evolved as have school systems—from simple to complex and from prescriptive to theoretical. Likewise, the models used and approaches taken regarding the knowledge base and delivery of programs have been evolutionary (see Murphy & Hallinger, 1987).

The emphasis on the development of a science of administration during the 1950s and the theory movement of the 1960s and 1970s have distanced preparation programs from the perspective of application. Risking oversimplification, the more recent approach taken by educational leaders has tended to emphasize *awareness training* as opposed to *skill building*. Our approach is to fuse the two.

The preparation of educational leaders is predicated on the assumption that the complexity of administration demands that leaders be adept in concepts and multiple knowledge areas. Professional groups, including member institutions of the University Council for Educational Administration (UCEA), have long deliberated the issue of the knowledge base in educational administration preparation. The approaches taken by the member universities, although somewhat varied in design and content, tend to reflect the belief that a variety of experiences enhance and enrich the acquisition of knowledge.

It is paramount that interns have opportunities to synthesize these experiences. The design of internship programs is diverse, but there is widespread agreement that internship is an integral part of the preparatory program.

However, there is an absence of agreement among those responsible for preparing aspiring educational administrators as to what should constitute the knowledge base as well as the scope and pattern of internship. Nearly three decades ago, Briner posited that the internship component existed "more as a result of chance than of careful consideration" (1963, p. 5). The definition, design, and content of internship remains under scrutiny. If professional competence is indeed founded on the acquisition of relevant knowledge and skills, the responsibility to inject meaning into the internship experience is critical. Bacilious (1987) posits:

> The models and practices in preparing and training members for full practice is in shambles, does not have an acceptable and appropriate theoretical base or body of knowledge and valid practical application, lacks in articulation of study and practice, does not have a well conceived internship experience. (p. 3)

One way of addressing the lack of articulation is to conceptualize a framework under which the elements of university coursework, field experience, and weekly seminars facilitate the formation of a professional knowledge base for interns.

The fundamental objective of the interns' professional preparation should be the acquisition of knowledge and skills that help them understand human behavior and adapt efficiently and effectively to varying circumstances. Ultimately, the aim is to improve the leadership abilities of individuals and educational systems. The internship itself provides for the assimilation and synthesis of experiences through the personalization and demonstration of purposive behaviors.

The focus of this chapter is on the selection of the knowledge base for an educational administration internship program. The discussion will focus on the knowledge base that informs educational leadership; where, how, and by whom knowledge acquisition can be provided; and considerations for packaging, sequencing, and synthesizing knowledge as campus-based content and field experiences.

WHAT CONSTITUTES THE KNOWLEDGE BASE?

The main concern in the development of any internship program is to provide a well-balanced experience that affords the intern an understanding of the role of the administrator. Given what is known about the tasks of educational administrators (see Greenfield, 1987; Murphy and Hallinger, 1987) and about the leadership abilities that administrators should possess (gleaned from research on effective schools), the task is then to determine what knowledge is of most worth and what experiences will most enhance acquisition and internalization of that knowledge.

A knowledge base for professional growth must, first and foremost, be aimed at informing and improving practice. This might best be perceived through the logic of cognitive psychology; that is knowledge is in the mind of the practitioner. To create an effective program, one must be able to select the appropriate knowledge to be incorporated in the program. In the case of educational administration, this means being able to select from general rules and principles underlying concepts such as leadership, decision making, problem solving, and conflict management (Cummings, 1989).

For many years the knowledge base in educational administration had as its source the disciplines of the social sciences. The social sciences were employed to improve the understanding of human organizations, including their functions, growth, and decline.

More recently, models such as those ascribed to by Schön (1983), Kolb (1984), Greenfield (1985), and others describe administration as "artistry rather than science." These models suggest not only "reflection-in-action" but "reflection-on-action"; that is, a metacognitive process involving the making of meaning out of experiences (Schön, 1983). Those aspiring to administration must gain skills in learning not only the "how" but the "what" and "why" in examining their experiences. All are necessary to be able to draw generalizations about future behaviors.

Several domains of professional knowledge are drawn on in differing degrees as demanded by the situation. When discussed relative to skills (or competencies), these domains are often couched in the language of technical, human, and conceptual skills.

> *Technical skills* refer to managerial proficiency in such areas as programming, scheduling, accounting, procuring, projecting, and assisting constituencies.
> *Human skills* include the part of administration that deals with the crucial tasks of decision making, problem solving, group processes, conflict resolution, and communication.
> *Conceptual skills* involve the ability to see the total enterprise as well as its parts, to understand interrelationships in complex situations, and to maintain a balance that promotes both unity and diversity.

According to Anderson (1989), these skills (shown in Figure 4.1) are best developed when ten knowledge domains are considered.

1. *Local knowledge.* This is knowledge that is specific to the setting, the community, and the organization. It is the "emic," the insider's knowledge or perspective. As Schön (1983) states, "when a manager reflects in action, he draws on this stock of organizational knowledge, adapting it to some present instance" (p. 242). Interns expand their local knowledge through exposure to different sites and personalities and hone their ability to use it

FIGURE 4.1: **Knowledge Domains and Skill Dimensions in Administrative Internship Programs**

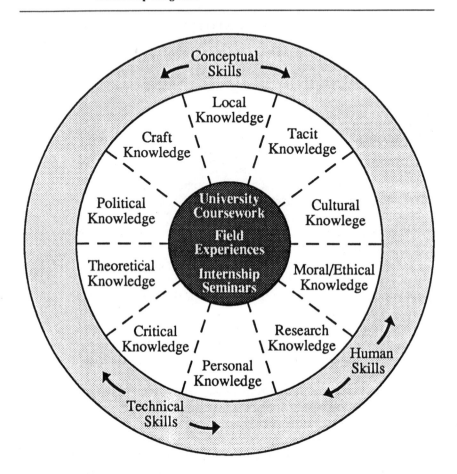

through discussing particular settings, communities, and organizations. This knowledge is a fundamental "tool kit"—perhaps not necessarily made use of daily, but always at hand.

2. *Tacit knowledge.* Polanyi (1958) describes this knowledge as much like intuition, known but difficult to express. Tacit knowledge in administrative practice involves both cultural and craft knowledge. If interns are encouraged to introspect on their actions and the actions of others, evidence of tacit knowledge emerges. Activities that examine the intuitive aspects of administrative behaviors and actions should be provided. Journals may reflect this in some depth, as may activities in problem solving and decision making.

3. *Cultural knowledge.* This domain may be defined as knowledge about the basic assumptions and beliefs that are shared by organizational members (see Schein, 1985; Sergiovanni & Corbally, 1984). Much of the literature on organizational culture stresses the importance of symbols, rituals, stories, and rites and the impact they have on the organization. It is, indeed, a knowledge base that can make the difference between being an effective or ineffective organizational leader. Without cultural knowledge, the administrator is predisposed to the lack of a shared vision. This knowledge is of utmost importance in creating and managing the assumptions and beliefs of a culture—some of which may be unconscious or semiconscious.

4. *Moral/ethical knowledge.* Moral/ethical knowledge affects decision-making situations in which moral dilemmas occur. Educational administrators must examine both individual and codified systems of ethics. Within and from this domain comes the building of platforms, beliefs, and philosophies. Problem-solving activities give interns an opportunity to examine the beliefs that undergird their own and others' thoughts, behaviors, and actions.

5. *Research knowledge.* Research data influence the practitioner's either directly or indirectly, affecting the ways in which educational organizations are conceptualized by those involved in organizational change. The intern must become an intelligent consumer of research in order to both analyze and influence decisions.

Research literature may be presented to and discussed with interns in a way that emphasizes the potential impact of findings. Intern activities aimed at reviewing and analyzing current research contribute to creating action-oriented educational leaders with a broadened sense of purpose.

6. *Personal knowledge.* Personal experiences, abilities, preferences, and styles have an impact on messages sent and received, decisions made, and knowledge acquired. In short, person-environment fit (French & Caplan, 1970) is critically important and must be considered to be a part of the knowledge base.

This personal dimension involves the discovery of ways to unite knowledge of the workplace with self-knowledge. When interns are given opportunities to introspect and reflect, a heightened awareness of self results. This awareness enhances the intern's ability to interact effectively with multiple and diverse constituencies.

7. *Theoretical knowledge.* "Theories-in-use" (e.g., Argyris and Schön, 1974) as well as "espoused theories" from the behavioral sciences act as templates for the development of individual beliefs, attitudes, and values about educational systems and the environments in which administrators function. Administrative interns must be given opportunities to examine behaviors relative to espoused theories. In addition, analyzing the impact of "what is said"

as opposed to "what is done" provides insight into valued attributes of leadership such as credibility and trust.

8. *Critical knowledge.* This domain may also be referred to as "critical reflection." This knowledge involves viewing administration from the perspective of the larger social system and the structures embedded in educational institutions. Leadership involves substantive issues, interpersonal interaction, and personal knowledge. Knowledge is maximized when interns are encouraged to connect problem analysis, planning, action, and reflection. Many other knowledge domains—such as local, political, cultural knowledge—are implicated. Interns must be given opportunities to examine and evaluate the critical elements involved in policies and programs from a global perspective.

9. *Political knowledge.* This area of knowledge is comprised of the awareness/knowledge of the power structures and networks of influence within the larger community as well as the educational organization. Interns need to become knowledgeable about the political dimension that impacts education. Opportunities can be provided to examine the impact of politics on education, from the politics of the classroom to that of the legislature.

10. *Craft knowledge.* Craft knowledge is based on professional experience: it is the repertoire of the practitioner. This domain goes beyond that of technical core operations to include reflective practice as well. It is important that interns be exposed to varied styles of leadership. Kolb's (1984) model of experiential learning may be used in discussing observations and perceptions. This model suggests a cyclical process of concrete experience, reflective observation, abstract conceptualization, and active experimentation. Through this reflective processing of experiences, knowledge can transcend technical expertise, making for excellence, not merely competence.

These represent the knowledge base on which aspiring administrators draw from consciously or unconsciously.

Figure 4.1 displays these knowledge domains and skill dimensions as a wheel. The three skill dimensions are influenced by the ten knowledge domains. For example, the domains of craft knowledge and skill areas are interrelated, that is, they bring together "art" and "science" of administration. The challenge is to devise experiences that provide and expand upon the domains of knowledge.

If students, school system leaders, and university faculty collectively participate in the identification and development of the knowledge base, it is likely that it will be meaningful and that broad-based support, or "ownership," will be created and maintained.

EXERCISE 4.1

Discussing the knowledge base

Questions that can guide the discussion include:

• What are the major skill areas to be included as perceived by (1) students, (2) school system leaders, and (3) university faculty members?
• What are the shared beliefs about the knowledge base in educational administration?

Figure 4.1 might be used to frame discussion of the knowledge base. How do participants perceive each knowledge domain? How does each knowledge domain influence the acquisition of skills. In planning academic coursework, internship seminars, and field experience focus should be directed toward how each of these domains can enrich the knowledge base. Participants may be encouraged to refer to related literature and to examine assumptions, state-mandated competencies, and other useful resources.

PROVIDING EXPERIENCES: WHERE, HOW, AND BY WHOM?

The design of the internship program can be represented by intersecting circles (see Figure 4.2): university coursework, field experiences, and weekly internship seminars. Figure 4.2 shows the interrelationship of the three elements and resulting knowledge. Each of the three elements affects and is affected by the other elements.

University Coursework

The guiding principle in selecting academic work is that it should have a direct bearing on practice. Thus coursework must be designed in such a way that it goes beyond mere knowledge dissemination and acquisition. More than simply acquiring knowledge, interns must master critical and analytical thinking if they are to effectively apply that knowledge in the real world.

There is no one best way to package academic coursework, but a guiding principle should be that its content reflect the knowledge base deemed important. This criterion can be used to guide the overall curricular design as well as the content and delivery of specific courses.

All domains of the knowledge base can be included in university coursework, but four in particular appear especially well suited: *Cultural knowledge, moral/ethical knowledge, research knowledge,* and *political knowledge.* To enhance

FIGURE 4.2: The Interrelationship of Elements in Administrative Internship

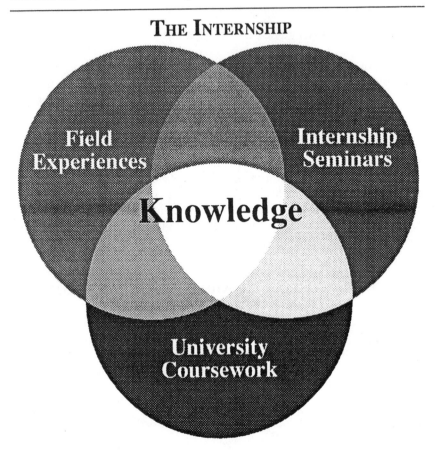

THE INTERNSHIP

Field Experiences

Internship Seminars

Knowledge

University Coursework

meaning and commitment, the planning, implementation, and revision of coursework requirements should include representatives from all interested/ affected constituencies. In the program planning stage, such a group can be formed to explore the aforementioned issues with respect to knowledge content and presentation formats.

EXERCISE 4.2
Considerations regarding university coursework

Groups may choose to meet and engage in brainstorming activities, which encourage members to be creative and innovative. Questions to be considered, and possibly grouped according to the themes listed in Figure 4.3, might include:

- What knowledge should be required?
- How should it be "packaged"?
- In what time segments should courses be offered?
- What nontraditional strategies and techniques for teaching should be considered—for example, required courses offered in blocks with teams of instructors each teaching their areas of expertise? Short modules? Student-led sessions?
- Should practitioners be considered as instructors? If so, for what courses?
- How can students be involved in planning course goals, objectives, and delivery?
- How can experiential work be included in coursework to parallel and enhance the intern's role in the field—for example, case studies, in-basket activities, and administrative simulations? What presently exists? What has to be developed?
- Should interns participate in courses as cohorts? What are the advantages and disadvantages?
- What courses taken at other universities or in other programs should be considered for credit?
- How can programs be individualized based on assessment center outcomes, stated needs, and career objectives (e.g. particular areas of concentration, course options, electives, tutorials, problems)?
- Should team management be promoted through providing opportunities to lead meetings and facilitate class sessions?

Program planners might also wish to examine how current academic coursework reflects the knowledge domains depicted in Figure 4.1.

Field Experiences

Field experiences allow interns to test academic knowledge against first-hand experience in administrative settings. Through observation of and involvement in decision making, as well as through reflection, self-testing, and guidance by the site administrator, interns can get a "feel" for the administrative role. In short, field experiences provide interns with opportunities to observe, judge, and accept or reject administrative behaviors (Briner, 1963).

Field experiences also demonstrate how academic knowledge relates to real-world practice. For example, the field experience can enhance existing *local knowledge* by exposing interns to different perspectives. *Tacit knowledge* is employed in decision making, problem solving, and conflict resolution and

FIGURE 4.3: Planning Matrix for Academic Courses

Academic courses	Time segements	Teaching strategies	Experiential work	Cohort opportunities	Planning of goals	Individualization personalization

is broadened by experiential interaction. *Critical, political,* and *craft knowledge* are intensified through involvement in site administration as well as in that of the larger organization. *Moral/ethical knowledge* comes into play as the intern observes ("or shadows") administrators at varied sites whose behaviors and demeanors differ, as well as through participation in problem-solving and conflict management activities. *Research* and *theoretical knowledge* domains are drawn upon in practical application and are contextually dependent.

It is at the field site that interns are challenged to internalize and personalize the knowledge that the program provides. Thus the field experience should be viewed as an integral component of the knowledge base. Through field experiences, interns can develop a global perspective on educational organizations and the role of administrators who lead them. If this is to occur, it is important that interns have opportunities to observe and be involved in a broad range of administrative functions.

In planning and organizing field experiences, those involved must decide which activities should be facilitated by district personnel and which can be complemented by university coursework and the internship seminar. It is also important that the field experience be conceived as a true internship—supervised advanced study in a professional field—not as an apprenticeship in which a trade is learned from the bottom up.

Representatives from the internship program staff, university faculty, school districts, and interns should be involved in planning field experiences.

EXERCISE 4.3

Planning the field experience

Program planners might brainstorm about the following questions:

- What knowledge acquisition and utilization can be best served by the field experience?
- What field experiences might amplify other elements of the program by providing an orientation to and understanding of the complexities of administrative roles?
- What types of field experiences would strengthen interns' human, conceptual, and technical skills?
- How can the field experience be designed and conducted so as to provide opportunities relative to the knowledge domains described by Anderson (1989)?
- What are the roles of the internship staff, field supervisors, and site administrators?

Once ideas are generated, planners might refer to Figure 4.1 to further discuss the role of the field experience in enhancing the skill dimensions and how opportunities may be operationalized.

Weekly Internship Seminars

The seminar serves several purposes. In the strictest sense, it is a time for introspection and discourse. It can also be the best way to synthesize coursework and field experiences.

Within the seminar, interns should encounter a variety of learning approaches, including diagnosis of site-based dynamics, analysis of cases, and role-play situations (see Appendix D for some sample cases). However, whatever the format, the seminar must maintain a balance between information dissemination and information processing. A good way to process experiences is through the use of a reflective journal.

Journals.   Keeping a reflective journal is one way for interns to examine their interactions from the viewpoint of an administrator and to determine the factors that an administrator must consider when making decisions. As Barnett and Brill (1988) state:

> Humans possess the unique ability to practice reflection by bringing past events to a conscious level, making sense of these events, and deciding how to act in the future based on what they have learned (p. 2.).

If field experiences are to enhance the knowledge domains, it is crucial that the relationship between the site administrators and the intern be supportive of knowledge development. Site administrators, in cooperation with university-based personnel, should encourage interns to reflect on their experiences and thus gain knowledge from them.

As Stager and Leithwood (1988) suggest, cognitive flexibility involves identifying sources of motivation (goals, moods, and expertise) and relating them to a person's action as mediated by characteristics of thought. In the arena of practice, the intern can examine these sources as applied to action and reflect and learn accordingly. From this perspective, learning is thinking and meaning centered.

Interns should be given ample time to synthesize their experiences and reflect upon them with colleagues. As alluded to earlier, the seminar should have a bearing on what is happening to interns in the field. By encouraging responsiveness and receptiveness, it should model what is expected of effective administrators.

Seminars can also enhance *professional knowledge* in the dialogue among the interns, capitalizing on their diversities in age, gender, ethnicity, education, experience, and aspirations. Through the seminars, interns can be kept abreast of current professional literature, conferences, conventions, and workshops (locally, regionally, statewide, and nationally) to expand their knowledge bases. These activities also serve to enhance interns' *political, craft, cultural,* and *local knowledge.* Interns should be encouraged to attend these functions in order to enhance their professional development via an increased awareness of "what's out there."

Autobiographies. Since personal knowledge can be a large part of the learnings in the internship seminar, interns can be required to complete autobiographies. Autobiographies are useful not only used for intern introspection but also as information sources that can help the program director and field supervisors provide the richest experience possible, given individual needs, strengths, and uniqueness. Birren (1987) describes the value of such an exercise in this way: "You don't know where you are going until you know where you have been. . . . In the hurrying and often bruising experiences of life, our uniqueness can get squeezed out like toothpaste from a tube, making us feel empty and discarded" (p. 91).

Seminars may also use various instruments and inventories to help students clarify their own personality types, communication styles, learning styles, and leadership styles. The value of these activities lies in validating the different styles, clarifying strengths, and enhancing self-knowledge.

EXERCISE 4.4
Planning the internship seminar

In conceptualizing and planning the seminars, the following questions might serve to guide a discussion:

- What are the goals of the seminar in terms of knowledge?
- Who should facilitate seminar sessions?
- What would be appropriate locations? Why (i.e., with what educational value relative to learning?)?
- What should be the content?
- What is an appropriate length and duration for seminars?

These questions and generated responses may be taken a step further to analyzing the influence of each in relationship to the knowledge domains. The matrix shown in Figure 4.4 may assist in this endeavor.

FIGURE 4.4: Planning Matrix for Internship Seminars

Goals/ Objectives	Content	Skill Areas	Knowledge Domains	Facilitation/ Leadership	Location/ Value

SEQUENCING COURSES, FIELD EXPERIENCES, AND INTERNSHIP SEMINARS

In part, decisions regarding sequence must realistically be based on such factors as availability of fiscal and human resources and local political considerations. In part, they should be based on one's conceptualization of learning and the ways it should take place. As discussed in Chapter 3, alternative ways of conceptualizing the sequence—linear, dialectic, reflective practice, and developmental (Milstein, 1990)—must be considered. Program planners must think through which approach would best serve their own particular purposes and needs.

IN CONCLUSION

The bottom line is that the knowledge base for intern programs must be viewed in its broadest possible sense. That is, knowledge should provide the foundation for effective leadership and should be gathered from multiple sources—ranging from site-based observations/experiences, to collegial interactions among interns, to academic coursework. Interns have learned how to bring diverse knowledge to bear in real-world situations. The nature of our task—that is, the preparation of leaders for our schools—requires us to take a global perspective as we attempt to define the knowledge base of our programs. Providing breadth and depth of opportunities and experiences in an internship is related to the kind of relationship that is established with role groups.

CHAPTER 5

Working Relationships Among School Districts, the University, and the Interns

ESTABLISHING AND MAINTAINING a cooperative working relationship among interns, school districts, and universities requires commitment throughout the development and implementation of the internship program. This cooperative partnership forms the cornerstone on which to build a successful program. The strength of this cornerstone rests on a high degree of trust among all parties. It also rests on a shared vision that working together in a partnership offers the best possibility of developing a meaningful preparation program for school leaders. Clearly written agreements concerning joint responsibilities, mutual benefits, and support help to develop the trust that must be present in successful partnerships. The needs of all participants must be addressed, and open lines of communication must be maintained among all members.

All of these relationships require team-building efforts that can be formalized through contractual agreements. This chapter focuses on this partnership-building process, including clarification of who the partners are, their contributions and responsibilities in building the partnership, the role of cohort development, and the contracts that formalize partnership agreements.

PURPOSES AND OBJECTIVES OF THE PARTNERSHIP

Clarification of purpose and specific objectives of a partnership should result in clearly defined statements that delineate the responsibilities and commitments of each party. These objectives should be established at three levels: university/district; program/site administrators; and, field supervisors/site administrators/interns.

University and District Officials. University and district officials are encouraged to form advisory boards to guide the partnership. A firm foundation for the internship can be laid by meeting together frequently in the formative stages to discuss concerns and issues. These initial meetings should focus on establishing the program's mission and goals and determining logistics and financial arrangements. Representatives from each participating institution should assist in the organization, promotion, and implementation of the partnership.

Program and Site Administrators. Program and site administrators form the second level of the internship partnership. These parties, in cooperation with universities and school districts, formulate site-relevant program objectives and activities as well as general time lines for achieving these objectives. These partners are key players in helping to prepare quality educational leaders.

Field Supervisors, Site Administrators, and Interns Field supervisors, site administrators, and interns need to create a reciprocal relationship in which all parties give and receive support and encouragement. This relationship can enable interns to receive individual attention and promote experiences that match their personal and professional goals. This relationship can further clarify and individualize activities by translating program goals into individual goals.

Cohort development among interns is also an important consideration. Cohort development promotes support and networking, and it helps interns create a more meaningful experience as group members. It can also assist individual interns in achieving their own professional goals. As such, this is an aspect that should not be left to chance.

CONSIDERATIONS IN FORMING A WORKING RELATIONSHIP

There are some basic issues of partnership development that must be addressed. These include the need to share common beliefs, determine roles, develop a nurturing environment, monitor progress, and build trust. These are all important facets of creating and maintaining partnerships.

Key Issues

Building trust may be a difficult task if parties have not collaborated on other projects or if past joint experiences have not been positive. Anticipating the possibility of future adversarial relations should be a strong incentive for partners to work to develop trust at the outset of the discussions.

Collaborative efforts by universities and school districts can be undermined by practitioners' mistrust of professors' motives. Professors are often perceived as being far removed from the "real world" and not particularly concerned about the schools' problems. This is an important message for professors to hear. As Land (1988) notes:

> What schools want, according to the informal feedback I get is help in dealing with real day-to-day problems that they are not able to solve very well. I believe that we [university professors] need the schools to help us maintain relevant preparation programs and that we can simultaneously contribute to problem solving in the schools. The potential for a viable partnership exists . . . But the success of such a venture depends upon all partners realizing worthwhile benefits from the enterprise and allaying feelings of being used. (p. 9)

Adequate time and consistent behavior are both required in the development of trust. Trust can also be enhanced through general understandings and appropriate facilitation of specific activities in the early stages of discussions between school districts and universities. The group membership should include such role players as superintendents, assistant superintendents, college of education deans, chairs of educational administration units, and faculty members. The internship program director, site administrators, and interns should also be included as participants in the discussion and planning of specific site-based activities.

Partnership-building activities can range from get-acquainted exercises, to discussions of common visions, goals, and expectations for the program, to activities that help remove barriers to communication. Exercise 5.1 below is one suggested way of accomplishing this objective.

When interns and site administrator partnerships have been determined, it may be useful to further explore teaming by examining characteristics regarding communication and leadership preferences.

EXERCISE 5.1
Personal responses to questions about team membership.

Responses to the questions listed below can be exchanged one on one, with each person taking a minute or two to share answers. To become better acquainted with others in the group, partners can be changed and new duos can discuss their respective answers. When the activity is complete, the facilitator might ask the group for overall reactions to the activity. Where clear agreements exist, norms can be developed. Where they do not, further discussion might be required. Sample questions include:

- Why do I think teams are beneficial?
- What is my philosophy regarding team membership?
- What are the roles and responsibilities that I would like to take on the team?
- What can I do to help build a strong team?
- How can I help resolve conflict on the team?
- How can I model good communication skills on this team?

Common Ground

An overall mission for internship programs can be established through identification of expectations. Partnership efforts frequently fail because common goals and professional interests are not shared, or at least are not recognized by the participants (Land, 1988).

Identifying common beliefs can be challenging because of the different perspectives of university and school district personnel. District personnel may feel that attention to the realities of educational administration—such as handling discipline, alcohol- and drug-related issues, building master schedules, working with parent groups, leading faculty meetings, developing budgets, and ordering textbooks—should take precedence over what they perceive to be the more "esoteric" topics that professors tend to dwell upon (e.g., leadership style, school climate management, and instructional improvement strategies).

The professors, on the other hand, may view the realities of schools through the lenses of theoretical and conceptual orientations. From their perspectives, educational administration involves examining such dimensions as organizational change, human resource management, and strategic planning from a frame of reference which goes beyond the "how-to."

Given these different perceptions, team-building activities are necessary to create an atmosphere conducive to problem solving and consensus building. Such efforts can help participants progress from identifying common beliefs to developing the program's mission. As a central element in the preparation of future educational leaders, intern activities must be given high priority in planning, lest it be overlooked in the myriad of details.

The discussion should go beyond the perceived role of the administrator as a business manager responsible for supervising personnel, budgeting, and organizing routines and procedures. Rather, it should focus on research findings that point to the importance of the administrator as instructional leader; that is, someone who is knowledgeable about and involved in the teaching and learning process of the school (Edmonds, 1979; Goodlad, 1983; Joyce, Hersh, & McKibbin, 1983; Lieberman & Miller, 1984; Mangieri, 1985; Rouche & Baker, 1986).

Many believe that in the future the teacher will be the instructional leader and the administrator, a facilitator (Carnegie Forum on Education and the Economy, 1986; Mitchell & Kerchner, 1983; Murphy & Hart, 1989). The concept of restructuring, whereby teachers are more involved in the decision-making process and in supervisory functions, has implications for the preparation of future administrators and, hence, the mission of administrator preparation programs.

Mutually Identified Needs

Partnership development efforts work best when the needs and interests of the partners are identified and supported. Thus, university and district partnerships should focus their mission statement on the goals of education and the roles of the administrator. Cooperative arrangements should be planned around specific and mutually identified needs. Wu (1986) identifies mutual needs and benefits, clear role expectations, conditions that are acceptable to all agencies, a functional communication network, administrative structures and support, trust, and selection of a process suited to the task as factors leading to success in collaborative projects.

Overcoming impediments to designing and implementing appropriate internship experiences is critical. This can be facilitated by discussing alternative approaches that fulfill the needs and purposes of the school districts, university, and prospective interns.

Identified needs will vary, ranging from school districts' interest in dealing with day-to-day situations, universities' interest in maintaining relevant preparation programs, and interns' interest in preparing for administrative positions. However, there is much common ground wherein satisfaction of one party's needs can also result in satisfaction of others' needs. Identifying this common ground is important in assuring that the needs of each part are met. Acting on the belief that the partners have equal and worthwhile needs and contributions to make can assure success for all involved.

BUILDING THE TEAM RELATIONSHIP: ROLES AND RESPONSIBILITIES

The roles and responsibilities of key players should be established early in the planning stages. A productive working relationship relies on all parties' understanding that their roles are crucial. As a jigsaw puzzle would be incomplete without all of its pieces, so a partnership without all members playing active and appropriate roles would be incomplete. This section focuses on the roles of key players: program director, field supervisors, site administrators, and interns.

The Program Director

The program director is the primary facilitator, catalyst, and organizer of the internship program. The importance of this individual in supporting interns and in bringing others together for planning, implementation, and evaluation cannot be overemphasized. The director must understand the role of the site administrator; serve as a positive role model and liaison among site administrators, interns, and field supervisors; facilitate operations; and protect the personal and professional interests of all parties. Above all, the director must be a strong student advocate. The nature of the position requires that the director be a confidant(e), friend, encourager, cheerleader, counselor, intermediary, guide, and disciplinarian.

The program director is usually the one to convene the partners, provide materials, plan meetings and strategies, oversee relationships, and provide the necessary follow-up and feedback required to maintain the partnership. The director is often responsible for facilitating meetings with site administrators and interns and outlining program expectations in concert with university and district personnel. It is the responsibility of the program director to monitor contractual agreements between the university and the district, as well as among field supervisors, site administrators, and interns.

Field Supervisors

Field supervisors are usually employed on a part-time basis to assist the director in supervisory duties. These supervisors can ensure that interns' experiences in the field are related to program objectives and are in compliance with the competency contract. They can also encourage the intern to reflect on experiences and gain knowledge from them. They can make an enormous difference by providing positive reinforcement that helps interns negotiate difficult situations.

It is important that the field supervisors meet regularly with the program director to discuss program and intern commendations, recommendations, evaluations, and strategies.

Site Administrators

Site administrators are key players in successful internship experiences. The recruitment and selection of these individuals should be carefully planned. How site administrators are chosen and monitored varies from program to program, ranging from self-selection to de facto involvement due to being administrators of those becoming interns, to being selected by district leaders. A well-justified argument for each approach can be made. All parties should agree on criteria for selecting field supervisors.

The site administrator's role as mentor involves a kind of "chemistry" or "fit" between two individuals. This kind of relationship exceeds the boundaries of teaching, leading, and supervising, which are thought to be the essence of an internship. Appendix A provides an overview of the desired characteristics of a mentors, a description of mentoring functions, a selected bibliography on mentoring, and a checklist of mentoring skills.

Mentoring relationships often result in long-term commitments to the personal and professional growth of the protégé(e). This does not mean that all relationships between site administrators and interns will evolve in this way.

Clearly, there are two kinds of site administrators in an internship—those who provide opportunities to attain the necessary skills as site administrators and those who go beyond imparting skills and knowledge to become mentors. All site administrators need to interact with interns to establish goals, provide experiences, monitor progress, provide access and resources, support accomplishments, and make recommendations. What distinguishes those who also become mentors is the view that their relationship with interns includes more than being a teacher and professional advocate. Recent attempts have been made to encourage mentoring based on formal, planned relationships (Frey & Noller, 1983). Regardless of whether relationships are planned or evolutionary, there is reciprocity in a true mentoring relationship.

Individual Interns

Administrative interns are at the center of the partnership. All efforts should be aimed at the development of individualized programs of study and field experiences that meet their needs and career aspirations.

Interns play a special role in the partnership. In reality, they are multiple role players. They often retain professional positions held prior to the internship, taking on intern activities in addition to these roles. Further, they interact frequently and on different bases with each of the other role players. Thus it is especially important that role expectations be clarified for the interns.

A learning cycle should be established wherein the intern starts with observations across the range of administrative functions. It is crucial that the intern become acquainted with all facets of the work of the site administrator and that the site administrator be observed in a variety of situations. These opportunities should permit the intern to learn about, or take part in, the development of policy and to have contact with the process of policy implementation.

The ambiguity and multiplicity of roles are further complicated through the passage of time, since interns begin as novices and progress to a fuller administrative perspective. The successful negotiation and resolution of this conflict situation can be enhanced through the development of a cohort.

The Intern Cohort

Considerable effort must be made to help interns develop ways of working together and becoming a close, supportive cohort group. This support is necessary if members are to succeed in an experience that is intense, demanding, and requires great commitment.

Cohort development helps interns become true colleagues. The need for a close, supportive cohort must be understood by all involved in developing an internship program, especially by the interns themselves. They need to know from the outset that they are an interdependent group and need one another's experience, abilities, and commitment to arrive at mutual and individual goals. Group members must be committed to the idea that working together can lead to more effective learning experiences than working in isolation. Group-building skills as well as good communication skills can be useful in this process. Reviewing these skills with interns can help them to become a cohort group and assist them as they prepare to work with many different groups as administrators.

The foundation for building this cohort is the selection process. As suggested by LaPlant, Hill, Gallagher, and Wagstaff (1989), it is helpful for groups to have a mix of gender and ethnicity and include suburban, urban, and rural district representation when possible. Such a mix provides for diversity when work groups or task groups are formed. Considerable insights can be gained through conversations about educational issues and potential solutions. Further, appreciation of the strengths and problems of different work environments can be gained through such sharing.

Some internship programs encourage cohort groups by bringing all interns together in a seminar. This provides extended contact with others who are at similar stages of advanced graduate study and enables students to interact with peers and faculty in ways that are typical of residency programs. This concept should be promoted if the program is seen as a clinically focused, professional model for the preparation of practitioners.

As a start towards cohort development, the program director might engage the interns in a discussion based on the questions posed in Exercise 5.2.

EXERCISE 5.2

Becoming a cohesive cohort group

The purpose of this exericse is to help the group clarify how it can become more cohesive. The group should review the following questions. After thinking about them individually, they can then explore them as a large group.

- What individual needs do we have that might be satisfied in the group?
- How can we increase the likelihood that these needs will be considered by the group?
- How can we improve the group's ability to meet these needs?
- How can we help other members of our group be assured that their needs are being considered by the group?
- What do we share as a group (e.g., activities, goals, procedures, beliefs)?
- How can we encourage each member to abide by group norms?
- How can we stimulate pride and satisfaction in the group for accomplishing challenging tasks?

CONTRACTUAL AGREEMENTS OF THE PARTNERS

It should be emphasized that the team-building activities already mentioned in this chapter should not be a one-time event. They cannot be accomplished through one or two workshops. Team-building activities require continuous, ongoing diagnosis, planning for implementation of change based on these diagnoses, evaluation of change efforts, and modifications of the program as indicated by the evaluation.

Roles and responsibilities can be initially determined in an informal way, but ultimately they should be formalized in a contract designed by all parties. A partnership is defined as "a legal relationship existing between two or more persons contractually associated as joint principals usually involving close cooperation between parties having specified and joint rights and responsibilities" (Webster's New Collegiate Dictionary, 1981, p. 836). This definition fits contract requirements for an internship program, which is a relationship in which the participants function collaboratively as equals in tackling problems for which there are not set answers (Hazlett, 1986).

These rights and responsibilities can be outlined in three types of contractual agreements that need to be developed in order to clarify expectations, guide practice, and bring focus to evaluations: university and school district contracts, site administrator contracts, and intern competency contracts.

University and School District Contracts

The university and school district contract should enumerate general expectations for all parties—university, school districts, and interns. The fiscal agreement between the school district and the university should be specified. As noted in Figure 5.1, contracts between universities and school districts should list general expectations and responsibilities of the university, school district, and the intern. All agreements should be approved by those in positions of authority, including members of the board of education and the district superintendent as well as those in similar positions at the university level.

Site Administrator Contracts

The site administrator faces both challenges and opportunities in working with interns. The opportunities lie in being able to make a significant

FIGURE 5.1:   Elements to Consider in a University and School District Contract

---

PART I   OVERVIEW OF THE CONTRACT
  A. Name of the university and school districts
  B. Dates and duration of the internship
  C. Number of interns
  D. Status of interns
     1. In the district
     2. In the university
  E. Logistics
     1. Absences and leaves
     2. Work assignments
  F. Contract termination and renewal

PART II   UNIVERSITY RESPONSIBILITIES
  A. Academic records of interns
  B. Procedures for selection of participants
  C. Employment conditions during the internship and upon completion
  D. Tuition payment and/or remission
  E. Supervision and authority patterns
  F. Fiscal arrangements and financial responsibilities

PART III   SCHOOL DISTRICT RESPONSIBILITIES
  A. Financial commitments and responsibilities
  B. Status of the role players

PART IV   COST PROPOSAL AND BUDGET
  A. Fixed costs of the program
  B. Variable costs of the program
  C. Summary of costs to districts
  D. Summary of costs and methods of collection and disbursement

---

contribution to the field of education. Since an intern's growth depends to a considerable degree on the model provided by the site administrator, certain responsibilities should be clearly outlined.

Clarification of ways the site administrator can involve the intern as a valuable contributor to the school operation and, at the same time, provide for the intern's mastery of important administrative competencies should be the intent of this contractual agreement. The site administrator contract should include the dimensions suggested in Figure 5.2.

Intern Competency Contracts

Competency contracts should be tailor-made to meet the individual needs of interns and promote a collaborative effort between site administrators and interns. They should include site-specific as well as career goals of the intern and be negotiated by the intern, site administrator, field supervisor, and program director.

The matrix shown in Figure 5.3 may be used to assist interns, site administrators, field supervisors, the program director, and university faculty in designing experiences and activities within each of the competency areas.

The contract should specify the competencies that the intern and site administrator can use as objectives for the field experience, based on research, state and local competency lists for administrators, practitioner experience, and the individual needs of interns. The contract should identify the field-based activities the intern will be involved in at specific sites. Figure 5.4 outlines important areas to consider including in the competency contract.

FIGURE 5.2:   Elements to Consider in a Site Administrator Contract

---

PART I   RESPONSIBILITIES OF THE SITE ADMINISTRATOR
   A. Assistance to the intern in becoming oriented to the total organization and the roles of various administrative positions
   B. Participation in the development of a competency contract that ensures breadth and depth of experience
   C. Provisions of opportunities to observe across the range of administrative functions
   D. Participation as a member of the internship team

PART II   ASSURANCE OF INTERN INVOLVEMENT IN A BROAD RANGE OF ACTIVITIES AND IN FULFILLMENT OF THE COMPETENCY AREAS
   A. Provisions to engage in the areas described in the competency contract
   B. Assignment in responsibilities that contribute to the school or enterprise
   C. Provision of opportunities to have full responsibility for a problem project that makes a significant contribution to the school or agency
   D. Time allowed to attend meetings and activities held for administrators and supervisors, and to observe in other schools and offices

---

FIGURE 5.3: Planning Matrix for Internship Experiences and Compentency Contracts

LEADERSHIP ROLES

LEADERSHIP ACTIVITIES	Instructional leadership	Communication	School Climate	Management of resources	Policy awareness
Planning					
Goal Setting					
Development					
Implementation					
Evaluation					

**FIGURE 5.4:   Suggested Areas to be Included in an Intern Competency Contract
                 and Their Related Activities**

INSTRUCTIONAL LEADERSHIP	MANAGEMENT OF RESOURCES
Curriculum	Human
Instruction	Financial
Supervision	Physical Plant
Research/Evaluation/	Equipment
Planning	Materials
	Programs
COMMUNICATIONS	Time
Informing	
Leading	POLICY AWARENESS
Encouraging and Initiating	Governance/Policy Making
Listening and Assisting	Law
Exploring and Recognizing	Community Relations
MANAGEMENT OF SCHOOL CLIMATE	*Evaluation for specific activities should*
Knowledge of Climate	*be delineated at the outset (e.g., for such*
Involvement and	*elements as curriculum development,*
Participation	*time management, etc.)*

A general list of competencies can be generated through a review of competencies published by national groups, state education agencies, local school districts, and effective schools research. It is highly recommended that interns be involved in the generation of competency contracts so that they meet their needs and a sense of meaning prevails. Competencies that cannot be fulfilled at a particular site may be acquired at other sites, suggested as seminar topics, or formulated as alternative activities.

Partners should jointly engage in an exercise to discuss ways to make the field experience meaningful. A suggested approach to this is described below in Exercise 5.3.

Inherent in all the categories of the contract is the expectation that planning, goal setting, implementation, and evaluation strategies will be developed. Ultimately they should be translated into individual education plans for interns, enabling them to achieve their individual goals as well as fulfill site-specific requirements.

An important facet of the competency contract is the unique opportunity it provides for intern, site administrator, field supervisor, and program director to plan for and openly discuss intern experiences. Without this information, important opportunities and insights may be minimized or lost. Frequent reviews of expectations and progress should be made based in part on weekly monitoring by field supervisors. The contract is intended to clarify intent and provide the basis for evaluation.

Continuous review sessions should be held throughout the process and revisions made when appropriate. These review sessions play an important role in building the joint responsibility for the interns' success.

EXERCISE 5.3
How can field experiences be meaningfully designed?

Each participant may be asked to think about this question from his or her particular perspectives and list as many opportunities as possible across the range of administrative functions. After individual lists are complete, small group discussions may follow before discussion takes place in the large group.

The discussion should include procedures for orienting the intern to the school district, the roles of various administrative positions, meetings and sessions for attendance, and the best way to incorporate these activities into the competency contracts.

IN CONCLUSION

This chapter has focused on the partnership-building process. Who the partners are, their roles in building the partnership, and the contractual agreements into which they enter have been detailed. Trust among all parties, as well as a common vision of the program's purposes and objectives, play an important role in this process.

All participants who are directly affected by the partnership should be included in the process of defining roles and responsibilities. This requires that they set aside adequate planning time to deliberate details regarding rights and responsibilities as well as the goals and objectives of the program; in addition, they need to agree on what evidence will be used to measure the achievement of these goals and support. Meaningful rewards and opportunities to meet individual needs must be provided for all participants in the partnership.

Just as in personal relationships, university and school district partnerships may suffer from unrealistic expectations: "Many a good idea in education has been junked, not because it lacked value, but because it could not meet all the expectations of it" (Hazlett, 1986, p. 192).

Problems are not unsurmountable. They can be resolved through common beliefs, defining roles and responsibilities, monitoring progress, and making adjustments. It is through trust that problems are solved and the possibilities increased that lasting partnerships can be created.

PART II

Follow-Up

CHAPTER 6

Placement and Follow-Up

THE GOAL OF MOST INTERNS is to obtain an administrative position. Their internship experiences should give them the skills and self-confidence necessary for such a career transition. But interns completing their programs also need activities that will help them search out and successfully compete for administrative positions.

This chapter focuses on these important tasks. Moving interns from preparation to practice should be a central theme running through the program. Interns need to learn how to build professional networks, assess their readiness, clarify their career preferences, and learn job-seeking skills. The program should include such activities as career planning; development of clear, accurate, and up-to-date pictures of the kind of administrative positions that may be available; and how to apply for them successfully.

CAREER PLANNING

Assessing Readiness for Seeking an Administrative Position

Well before searching for an administrative position, interns should be encouraged to assess their readiness for this activity. There are a number of specific things that need to be considered, many of which are listed in Figure 6.1, a self-assessment that can help interns clarify their readiness for the transition into management. This self-assessment might be assigned at the end of one seminar session, with interns asked to reflect on it before the next session, when it will be discussed.

This will be the first experience for most interns in finding an administrative position. What is obvious to "veteran" administrators is probably not to those who are entering the job market for the first time. Given this, it would be helpful to introduce this exercise at the outset of the program (as suggested in Chapter 2), when interns should be thinking about what is required to find a position, and then again near the end of the program, when this activity will become a dominant concern.

FIGURE 6.1:   Inventory for Assessing Job Placement Readiness

	DEGREE OF READINESS		
TOPICS	Far to go	Making progress	Pretty close
1. Certification/licensure completed	——	——	——
2. Administrative role preference clear	——	——	——
3. Geographical preference clear	——	——	——
4. Able to obtain good recommendations from administrators and professors	——	——	——
5. Good sense of job market	——	——	——
6. Good interviewing skills	——	——	——
7. Résumé developed, critiqued, and up-to-date	——	——	——
8. Networks established with educational leaders	——	——	——
9. Sponsorship established with administrators and professors	——	——	——

Career Directions

Career planning should begin as early as possible to assure the widest possible choice once interns actually begin to search for administrative positions. As one of the first activities in their programs, interns would benefit greatly from some introspection about alternative directions their careers might take. To do so, interns might be asked to respond to the questions in Figure 6.2 (as suggested in Chapter 2). It would then be helpful to repeat the exercise near the end of the program, with interns comparing their responses with those made at the beginning. They should look for similarities and differences and think about the implications for career planning.

The comparisons could be reviewed and analyzed individually, in tutorials, or in a seminar session. Discussing with others can lead to further insights that might be helpful in career planning. Specifically, interns might benefit from exploring the following questions:

• How consistent are the earlier/more recent responses?
• What has changed? Why?
• What changes have taken place that have immediate and direct implications for the intern's career plans (e.g., priority short- and long-term role choices, geographic considerations, salary expectations)?
• What is the intern presently doing to achieve his or her career goals?
• What additional things should the intern begin to do?

FIGURE 6.2: Preliminary Internship Questionnaire

---

1. Why did you apply to this program?

2. Are you interested in obtaining an administrative position? (If yes, please continue.)

3. How soon after you complete the program do you expect to obtain such a position:
   —— A.   Immediately following the program
   —— B.   Within a year or two
   —— C.   Sometime in the future

4. How would you feel about moving to a new location to obtain an administrative position?

5. If you would move, what limits, if any, do you place on such a move (e.g., type of community, geographical regions that are acceptable)?

6. Can you specify what administrative role(s) you would like to obtain when you complete the program?

7. How long do you expect to stay in your first administrative position?

8. What administrative role would you like to advance to as a second position, and how long do you expect it would take you to make this second move?

9. What "ultimate" role(s) would you like to obtain and why?

10. How much do you expect to earn during your first year in administration? How about ten years later?

The point of the exercise is straightforward; that is, the more interns can clarify their aspirations and needs regarding roles, settings, salary, and so on, the more they will be able to set an effective course toward finding an appropriate administrative position. Without this kind of introspection and discussion, they will find themselves following leads wherever they might be and, possibly, committing themselves to positions that do not fit well with their dispositions and preferences.

Networking

A critically important part of interns' career planning is networking, both for the contacts it creates and for the clarification it provides regarding alternative paths to the kinds of positions they might want to pursue. By expanding vision and promoting discovery of what works through observing role models who compose one's network, the *what you know* part of qualifying for administrative positions is enhanced. Equally important, networking expands the *who you know* part of finding appropriate positions. It is therefore important for the staff to help interns create and expand networks of professional relationships.

The first question is *who* should be considered as potential members of the network? Obviously key educational leaders from one's own school district should be cultivated. They possess knowledge about the workings of the district and can exert influence on behalf of aspiring administrators. But the network should also be expanded to include key educational leaders from neighboring districts as well as from across the state, if not the nation. For one thing, interns may someday find themselves looking for positions outside their own school districts. Equally important, ideas and innovations so necessary to the ultimate educational effectiveness of our schools are likely to be found in other educational settings. In addition to site administrators, the network should include educational policy makers in such units as intermediate educational systems, state departments of education, and professional associations.

The second question to consider is *how* to develop the network, a new activity for most interns. It must be undertaken with seriousness of intent and an approach which slowly but effectively builds a solid base of networking relationships. We recommend that an approach similar to the following series of steps be explored by the staff and the interns:

1. *Clarify networking purposes.* At an early internship seminar the staff and interns should discuss the meaning and value of networks. For example, the concept might be defined, the initial role players identified, and a logical

sequence of networking development strategies agreed upon. The staff and interns might discuss ways they can pool their knowledge of key role players who could be approached to become part of the network. In addition, where appropriate, tasks and responsibilities for this activity can be assigned.

2. *Get feedback on the approach.* Administrators, field supervisors, site supervisors, and university faculty members in educational administration might be invited to respond to the strategies and make recommendations for changes as necessary. Of course, these individuals should also be viewed as potential initial members of the developing network. To allow time for adaptations, this activity should begin early in the program.

3. *Expand the network and evaluate progress.* Throughout the interns' program the networks can be expanded as interns interact in field settings, attend professional meetings, and are exposed to exceptional leaders during their academic course work and internship seminars. Occasional formal reviews of the status of interns' networks both by interns individually and by the staff working with them can help keep this activity on track.

4. *Review outcomes.* Near the end of the program, a review of the status of interns' networks can be useful. Perhaps a closing internship seminar can be organized that brings interns and key educational leaders together to assess the situation. Topics might include job possibilities that appear to exist in the area, leaders who can be of assistance in putting interns in contact with appropriate job sites, identification of deficits, and clarification of ways that these networks can be expanded.

It should be remembered that networks are a form of support group. As such, they should be built on the premise that members will provide mutual assistance (Lipnak & Stamps, 1982). In other words, it goes both ways: Aspiring administrators must be prepared to provide support in whatever ways they can to members of their professional networks if they expect to be supported by them. Unless this basic principle is honored and practiced, the results of networking are likely to be minimal or possibly even negative.

FINDING THE RIGHT JOB

Before beginning to look for administrative positions, interns should have a sense of *what's out there*. This includes knowing what kinds of administrative positions exist, what the demographics are regarding who fills these positions and what the compensation levels might be. It also means knowing how to find out about specific job openings.

Positions

As Figure 6.3 catalogs, there are many different kinds of administrative positions, at least in larger, more comprehensive school districts. While many interns will probably obtain their first administrative positions as assistant principals or principals, it should not be assumed that these are the only entry-level positions available. Nor should it be assumed that a successful administrative career is linear and limited to advancement from building level to superintendency. There are many administrative specialities that can be explored, both at the outset and later in one's administrative career. Too often interns have an unnecessarily narrow perspective concerning positions that might be available to them as they begin their administrative careers.

Interns are encouraged to learn about the different kinds of administra-

FIGURE 6.3: Typical Educational Administration Positions

SUPERINTENDENT

ASSOCIATE/ASSISTANT SUPERINTENDENT

DIRECTORS:
Finance/Business
Instruction/Curriculum
Special Education
Personnel
Pupil Services
Maintenance/Building/Grounds
Planning
Public Relations
Research and Evaluation
Transportation
Professional Development
Technology/Computer Education
Activities
Athletics
Media Services

SUPERVISORS OF MAINTENANCE:
Plumbing
Electrical
Heating and Air Conditioning
Vehicle Maintenance

COORDINATORS:
Accounting
Payroll
Purchasing
Warehousing
Custodial Services
Elementary/Secondary Education
Certified/Noncertified Personnel
Speciality Areas in Special Education
Counseling/Guidance
Psychological Services

PRINCIPALS/ASSISTANT PRINCIPALS

EDUCATION SPECIALISTS

HEALTH AND NURSING SERVICES

BUSINESS-RELATED POSITIONS:
Finance
Real Estate
Purchasing

---

tive positions that exist in their geographic areas of interest. In addition to increasing the number of applications they can make, they will also expand their perceptions of career choices and thus be better able to establish the most appropriate fit between their strengths/interests and the administrative positions that may be available.

While it is not likely that first-time candidates will compete successfully for a superintendency in most districts, it is possible that they will do so for director, coordinator, specialist, and business-related positions.

Demographics

Interns should also have a sense of where the jobs are and who currently fills various positions. Heller and Conway (1988) conducted a nationwide survey that provides important information concerning this question (see Figure 6.4). Some of the most important points are summarized here.

1. *Gender.* Educational administration is still a predominantly male profession. However, this is likely to change dramatically as those with many years of service retire and those presently being trained move into administrative positions. Whereas males represented most of those who were preparing for administrative roles prior to the 1980s, females are now the majority group in most preparation programs.

2. *Race.* The field is still predominantly white. However, in recent years extraordinary efforts have been made, at all levels of government, to identify members of minority groups who can fill administrative positions. In fact, in many areas of the country, minorities are finding themselves being aggressively recruited to fill administrative positions.

3. *Location.* Less than half of the administrative positions available are in suburban and urban areas. Further, one-quarter of the positions are in districts with enrollments of less than 1,000 students, and 70 percent are in districts with enrollments of less than 5,000 students. Those who are looking for their first position should recognize that they will be narrowing their possibilities by at least half if they insist on finding a position in a metropolitan area. Equally important, positions in rural areas and small towns will likely provide a wider scope of experience and learning for first-time administrators than will those in metropolitan areas where school systems are usually much larger and administrative roles are likely to be more narrowly defined.

FIGURE 6.4:   A Portrait of School Executives

SCHOOL EXECUTIVES AT A GLANCE

	Princi-pals[1]	Central Office Personnel[2]		Princi-pals[1]	Central Office Personnel[2]
Sex			Highest degree earned		
Male	83.%[3]	93.%[3]	Bachelor's	1	1
Female	17	7	Master's	62	37
Race			Specialist	25	27
White	91	97	Doctorate	13	36
Black	5	2	Length of service in		
Hispanic	3	2	education		
Other	2	—	5 years or less	—	1
Age			6-10 years	4	—
Under 30	—	—	11-15 years	18	8
36-41	7	1	16-20 years	24	19
42-47	26	27	21-25 years	18	26
48-55	31	31	26-30 years	20	21
56-64	13	27	More than 30 years	16	26
Over 65	2	—	Years in current position		
Community[4]			1 year or less	5	8
Rural	28	24	2-3 years	26	25
Small town	30	26	4-5 years	13	19
Suburb	25	35	More than 5 years	56	48
City	17	15	Age at which planning		
Enrollment[4]			to retire		
Less than 1,000	26	20	55 or younger	24	16
1,000-4,999	43	45	56-59	35	31
5,000-9,999	8	15	60-64	29	40
10,000-24,999	11	10	65-69	10	12
More than 25,000	12	9	70 or older	2	2

[1]Includes elementary, junior high/middle school, and high school principals.
[2]Includes district superintendents and deputy, associate, and assistant superintendents.
[3]Not all columns total 100% because of rounding.
[4]The district superintendents in this example represent a slightly different mix: 37% work in rural communities, 28% in small towns, 24% in suburbs, and 10% in cities; 41% head school systems with enrollments of less than 1,000 and 42% with 1,000-4,000.

Source: Reprinted, with permission, from *The Executive Educator* (September 1987) Copyright © 1987, the National School Boards Association. All rights reserved.

4. *Degrees.* Most administrative positions are held by those with at least an M.A. degree. Further, more than a third of central office positions are held by individuals with a doctorate. The implications for continuing formal academic preparation beyond that required for an entry-level position are clear.

5. *Prior experience.* Most administrative positions are held by individuals with at least eleven years of service in education. For central office personnel the years of service are even higher. The point is that there are expectations for a broad experiential base before one is to be taken seriously as a candidate for administrative positions.

6. *Job duration.* About half of present administrators have stayed in their current positions for more than five years. While there is room for career advancement, aspiring administrators can anticipate that they will probably have to "serve their time" before pursuing alternative administrative positions.

Compensation

Often those applying for their first administrative position are shocked to find that they may actually have to take a significant decrease in salary. This is particularly true of senior teachers who have served for upwards of fifteen to twenty years. Many school districts have taken note of this problem and have instituted policies that are minimizing, if not eliminating, it. However, there will still be times when an aspiring administrator has to cope with this dilemma before deciding whether to accept a position.

While this must ultimately be an individual decision, one should not focus on entry-level salary alone. The quality of work life is a major factor that should be considered. Those who self-select into preparation programs for administrative careers are likely to be expressing a need for the challenges and opportunities of professional growth that such positions might provide. If there is a small loss of income, this might be a reasonable price to pay for staying energized professionally. Further, as one remains in administration and moves into higher positions, short-term income deficits are likely to be eliminated. Those who show promise as administrators will find financial advantages, although it may take time to be realized.

It is difficult to predict how much the first administrative position will pay, given that salaries will vary depending on specific administrative roles and on urban/suburban/rural and regional variations. However, there are some predictable remuneration ranges that can be offered as guidance. Heller and Conway's 1988 survey found that:

Principals report salaries from a low of less than $30,000 (9 percent) to a high of between $70,000 and $74,999 (less than 1 percent); more than 75 percent earn between $30,000 and $50,000 a year. For central office executives (including district superintendents, deputy, associate, and assistant superintendents), the range is greater—though none of the respondents in this survey reported incomes of more than $100,000. Few central office executives (1 percent) earn less than $30,000; the highest salary reported in this survey was between $90,000 and $94,000. . . . Three-quarters of all central office executives responding to this survey report earning between $40,000 and $70,000. (p.21)

Identifying Available Administrative Positions

The following are four sources of information regarding the availability of positions that aspiring administrators can explore.

1. *School district listings.* Most school districts post position openings. Consult the personnel office (or its equivalent) on a regular basis to stay informed.

2. *Placement offices of universities.* Universities maintain listings of interested employers, including school districts. Students who establish files with their university placement offices will be apprised of employment opportunities. When requested, most placement offices will send applicants' files to potential employers. In addition, for a nominal fee many will extend these services to individuals who are not students at that institution. This permits candidates who are willing to make a geographic move to be considered for position openings throughout the state and, if desired, in other regions of the country.

3. *The educational administration unit.* Many educational administration units maintain a file of available administrative positions. It is a good idea to peruse it on a regular basis when exploring job opportunities. In addition, most of these units keep in contact with educational leaders in their area, and some aggressively seek to help their students by making appropriate connections and recommending them to potential employers. Some also maintain contact with their graduates and help them to advance their administrative careers. Interns should find out how their educational administration unit perceives its role in this effort. In fact, if the unit does not presently take an active role in finding positions for its students, interns might encourage it to do so.

4. *Informal networks.* Here is where the effort to establish networks (noted earlier in the chapter) will pay off. If those in the network view candidates positively, they can be approached and asked for their assistance. They

can be helpful both by identifying available administrative positions and acting as interns' sponsors with those responsible for filling these positions.

GETTING THE PAPERWORK IN ORDER

When will interns be ready to actively seek positions? Several things should be attended to prior to making such an application. These include completing certification (in some states referred to as licensure) requirements, developing a concise and appropriate résumé, and preparing other written materials.

Certification

Completion of an academic program does not automatically assure completion of certification requirements. Whether there is a match between academic/clinical preparation and state certification requirements depends on particular universities' program designs. In addition, most states have requirements beyond academic training, such as a minimum number of years as a classroom teacher (perhaps even at a specific educational level—elementary or secondary—if administrative certification is by level) and completion of specific academic degrees. Aspiring administrators must know about their state's requirements and plan to fulfill them.

This can be done by writing the state education department, asking for certification requirements, and then checking with university advisers to see if they are all included in the program of studies. If not, additional state-required courses can be taken. It is best to know this at the beginning rather than risk the possibility of not having a certificate when searching for administrative positions. If a move to another state is a possibility, follow the same procedure (see Appendix B for a complete list of addresses of state education departments as well as the addresses of key national professional organizations that might be of help to those searching for positions).

Being certifiable upon completion of the academic program is an important foundation for subsequent job searches. It is possible to seek temporary waivers, but without certification completed, potential opportunities will be lost because interns will be competing with other candidates who will have their certification documents in order.

Résumé

A résumé is nothing more than a summary of an applicant's professional history, including employment, education, and other achievements. This summary is normally the first information that potential employers will receive, and it is all they will initially know about the candidate. The résumé should be constructed with great care. If it is not, it will probably be the last exchange that the candidate has with potential employers.

There is no one best way to construct a résumé, but there are some basic principles that should be followed:

- *Be brief.* Reviewers will likely have many résumés to review. As such, they cannot spend an inordinate amount of time on any one résumé. Equally important, they will be concerned with the candidates' ability to summarize their experiences concisely, because this is an early indicator of their ability to write successfully—that is, succinctly—as administrators. For these reasons résumés should be no more than a few pages long.
- *Let the facts speak for themselves with no editorial commentary.* Simply list achievements. Do not describe them in great detail. For example, list being a department chair but avoid describing all the duties the role entailed. This keeps the résumé brief. It also lets the reader know that candidates are confident that accomplishments will speak for themselves.
- *Include specific sections.* Different categories—such as education, work experiences, any honors, and relevant publications—should each be listed as separate sections. Within each it is advisable to list the most recent element first and then list the remainder in reverse chronological order.
- *Review and modify the résumé as necessary.* It is important to make the best case possible. This means updating résumés to include position changes, professional recognitions, achievements, additional coursework, and professional development activities. It also means modifying the contents to fit the specific job applied for. Learn as much as possible about the specific position and construct the résumé to emphasize strengths that match that role.
- *Prepare the résumé professionally.* The appearance of the résumé is important, since it is likely to be the first opportunity the candidate will have to impress potential employers. Therefore, it should be reviewed for style, presentation, and contents. It may also be worth the time and expense to seek professional counsel on the construction and production of the résumé and have copies run off on colored (e.g., off-white, beige, or light gray), quality bond paper.

Most aspiring administrators will have had little experience in constructing a résumé. Given the importance of this activity, it would be time well spent for the staff and the interns to explore issues related to the development of résumés in the internship seminar. The following steps can be quite helpful in résumé development:

1. Discuss the purposes and importance of résumés at a session early in the program.
2. At the same session, present a variety of sample résumés (both strong and weak) from which students might learn.
3. Conclude the session by asking each intern to develop a résumé and bring it to a later session for critiquing. Have interns rewrite their résumés on the basis of these critiques.
4. If possible, ask an "expert" or two (e.g., administrators who are noted for their insights about résumés, or specialists whose business it is to help job applicants prepare résumés) to provide feedback and suggestions for improvement. This might best be done after interns have developed several drafts of their résumés.
5. After redrafts are completed, ask a panel of personnel directors to review sample student résumés and provide feedback that can help them to strengthen their résumés.

Interns should be encouraged to use word processing and store their résumés on a disk (with back-up copies!) where they can be available for appropriate changes and updating as required. Having résumés stored on computer disks can help interns respond to job opportunities as they arise.

Résumés, as emphasized, are important elements in preparing for job searches. As such, interns are strongly encouraged to take this task seriously. To help them with this task, some useful books on résumé development are noted in the bibliography (Lewis, 1989; Parker, 1988; Smith, 1987; Yates, 1988).

Other Written Materials

In addition to résumés, aspiring administrators need to consider developing or obtaining other supportive documents. If these are appropriately designed and readily available, they can contribute greatly to finding a position.

Philosophy/Purposes/Platform. The educational reform movement has led to the justifiable conclusion that the potential for educational effectiveness is directly related to the existence of superior educational leadership. The educational effectiveness literature (e.g., Edmonds, 1979, and Sergiovanni, 1984) concludes that to be effective, educational leaders must have a sense of *purpose* (i.e., a vision of where they feel that education should be going), an *educational philosophy* (i.e., a set of beliefs about what a meaningful educational experience entails), and a *platform* (i.e., a design, plan, or set of directions of how one's philosophy and purposes can be instituted). Many school districts are now asking applicants to demonstrate that they have a sense of vision and purpose and that they have some ideas regarding how these will eventually be achieved. Sometimes a written statement of purposes or philosophy may be required. At other times such questions may come up in interviews. Given these possibilities, candidates should give considerable thought to clarifying their educational platforms and putting them in writing so that they are prepared to respond with confidence.

Additional Evidence. Some potential employers will ask for supportive evidence regarding such dimensions as writing style and ability, successful curriculum development, and experiences in extracurricular areas. These possibilities should be anticipated and developed as written resource files. When requested, they should be as professional in appearance as the résumé itself.

References. There are two kinds of references. One is the reference letter that speaks about a candidate's general potential. General references can be collected and kept on file for use as needed. For example, this type of reference should be included in the candidate's placement file at the university. The other type of recommendation focuses on the candidate's abilities as they relate to specific administrative positions. These may be requested at the time of application. When asking for letters of reference, candidates should provide their referees with information about the kinds of accomplishments and potential they might want to consider including when writing their statements. Most referees will appreciate such guidance, assuming that it is not offered too aggressively and room is left for their individual styles and initiative. Finally, while it may appear obvious, it cannot be overemphasized that great care should be taken in selecting referees. Candidates should be sure to pick those who feel positive about their potential as administrators. They should also be sure that their referees have outstanding reputations as well as relevant experience (e.g., in the present instance, as an administrator or a professor of educational administration).

HOW TO APPLY FOR POSITIONS

A candidate spends only a small amount of time with a potential employer. In that short span the candidate must be able to convince those making judgments that she or he is the right person for a particular administrative position. Nothing should be left to chance in creating a positive impression. Prior thought should be given to dressing appropriately, managing the interview situation effectively and, increasingly, performing well in behaviorally anchored assessment centers.

Appropriate Attire

The initial opportunity to impress comes before the first words are spoken. Clothing selected for application activities establishes an impression and sets the tone for all that follows. In general, dressing appropriately means reflecting the way that people are expected to dress in the work environment. Typically this means suits for men and dress suits for women, in subdued rather than brilliant colors, and, for both, hair that is well groomed. In all possible ways extra effort should be made to present a physical appearance that reflects professional norms. Significant deviation from these norms can set a negative tone from which it may be difficult to recover. Because attire and appearance are critical to the first impression, it would be worth reviewing a clothes guidebook (see Malone, 1975, 1977).

Interviewing Skills

In many cases the interview (or interviews, depending on the practices of particular school systems and the kind of position under consideration) may provide the only opportunity to make a positive impression. Given the importance of this event, it is surprising how many applicants go into an interview without preparing thoroughly for what might occur.

The job interview is *not* just another conversation among two or more adults. It is a focused and complex interaction that requires skill and concentration. Interviewers are usually well trained and will probably have much more experience with this kind of situation than will applicants.

Interviewers look for cues that lead them to positive or negative judgments. In all probability they will be looking for the degree to which candidates communicate clearly, respond to difficult questions effectively, demonstrate self-confidence and, in general, are able to manage the stress of the interview situation. Keeping this in mind, candidates should prepare well.

As with résumé preparation, there is much that can be done within the preparation program to help interns conduct themselves well in job application interviews. The following set of sequential ideas are offered for consideration:

1. Prior to the time that interns begin applying for positions, the staff can go over the guidelines for interviewing. Past experiences, positive and negative, should be shared and recommendations developed on the basis of these experiences.
2. Personnel directors from local school systems might be asked to join a seminar session to share their views about interviewing and answer any questions that interns may have.

3. Mock interviews can be held to rehearse and modify behaviors as well as to learn new techniques, perhaps conducted by administrators and/or school board members who have interviewed job applicants and can provide helpful feedback. Videotaping mock interviews can also allow for more relaxed review and later feedback. If other interns attend these mock interviews, they can provide relevant feedback as well as learn much from the experience. If time permits, the process can be repeated to capitalize on initial learnings and provide other interns the opportunity to be interviewed.
4. Finally, a synthesis session can be held to summarize key points, review learnings, and identify additional activities that specific interns might want to pursue.

It would also be profitable to hold discussions that focus on basic skills required for successful interviewing. Some useful skills that might be explored include the following.

1. *Learn about the position, the organization, and the environment.* Candidates should do their "homework" so they can speak intelligently about the specific role and the local setting. Interviewers will be positively impressed by the fact that candidates have such knowledge, and candidates will be better able to pick up cues from interviewers' questions. Candidates should read relevant written materials (e.g., organization documents, newspaper articles, etc.) and talk to knowledgeable individuals before going to the interview.

2. *Learn about the interview situation prior to the actual event.* Candidates will feel much more at ease if they know something about such basic things as the setting, the physical arrangements, the interviewer's role in the organization, and the length of the interview.

3. *Get to the interview early.* Candidates should arrive about fifteen minutes early so that they can relax and organize their thinking. This also ensures that they will be on time, an attribute that impresses interviewers positively.

4. *Behave with confidence in the interview situation.* Because the interview is for a leadership position, a high degree of self-confidence will be expected of the applicant. Interviewers are interested in *how* candidates conduct themselves as much as they are in *what* is said. Candidates impress interviewers if they show self-confidence, give due consideration to such things as correct physical posture, project their voices in ways that are engaging, and make frequent eye contact. If there is a group of interviewers, candidates should be sure to focus on each individual at one time or another during the interview. In addition, it is important to offer a firm handshake at the outset and at the conclusion of the interview.

5. *Answer questions directly and to the point.* Avoid providing more infor-

mation than interviewers request. Rather than being impressed by the depth of a candidate's knowledge, they will probably be dismayed by his or her inability to demonstrate an important administrative skill—knowing how to answer a question succinctly. Further, if the candidate does not have an adequate answer to a question, he or she should admit it. It is much better to admit lack of knowledge than to try to fake it. Interviewers are more positively impressed by candidates who are candid than by those who hedge and try to circumvent a question. A moment's consideration before responding is quite appropriate, given the dynamics of the situation. Reflecting before speaking is certainly preferable to hemming and hawing while trying to collect one's thoughts.

6. *Ask questions.* Toward the end of an interview, candidates may often be asked whether they have any questions. In fact, they might even take the initiative to do so. Candidates will impress interviewers positively if they seek information about the nature of the positions for which they are applying and about the overall organization in which they might be working. This shows both seriousness of intent and an ability to think as a leader. Candidates may also want to ask questions about such job conditions as salary range and fringe benefits, but they would do well to minimize such kinds of questions to avoid being viewed as focusing on self-interests. It is more appropriate to explore such questions when the candidate is invited to take a position.

7. *Help interviewers close the session on time.* There will probably be a fixed interviewing schedule. Help interviewers to stay on schedule (e.g., do not press for continuing discussion when the allotted time is up). The candidate should leave interviewers with a positive closing impression. This will be jeopardized if interviewers feel that the candidate is obstructing the flow and the interview is going beyond the allotted time. Of course, if interviewers encourage candidates to remain beyond a given time, they should take advantage of the opportunity.

Assessment Centers

Recently school districts have begun to question whether interviews, résumés, and references provide a sufficient basis for decision making regarding employment of administrators. They are important, but they do not provide potential employers with opportunities to make behavioral observations that predict how candidates will actually perform on the job.

To compensate for this shortcoming, assessment centers, initially developed for use in government agencies and later in business and industry, are being adopted as part of the administrator selection process by school districts (see Milstein & Feidler, 1989). Assessment centers provide behaviorally anchored data by putting candidates through a variety of experiences in which their management abilities are observed and assessed. For example, assessments are made of candidates' abilities to solve problems, make decisions, deal with conflict, and work in team situations.

One of the most heavily publicized assessment center approaches, the Principals Assessment Center, has been developed by the National Association of Secondary School Principals. However, in an attempt to reduce the time and costs that the Principals Assessment Center entails, many school districts have modified it or are developing their own assessment centers.

The best way to help interns prepare for an assessment center is to be sure that there are comparable experiences in the preparation program. In fact, as noted in Chapter 3, it is recommended that an assessment center be part of the initial intern selection process. In the preparation program itself, there should be many opportunities for active learning by experiencing such things as role playing, case studies, simulations, in-basket exercises, and making formal presentations. Interns who have such experiences will likely do well if they encounter an assessment center in their job searches.

IN CONCLUSION

This chapter has focused on helping interns to identify and apply for administrative positions. Careful planning, preparation of appropriate materials, and learning of necessary skills are all required to locate and obtain an appropriate position. In short, it is an activity that should not be left to chance. Rather, it should be considered as an integral part of interns' programs and begin during the earliest phases of these programs.

CHAPTER 7

Evaluating Interns and the Internship Program

EVALUATION LETS US KNOW how close we have come to meeting our purposes and provides information needed to make decisions that can improve our performance. As such, it is an important aspect of the planning and management of internship programs.

There are two major evaluation purposes that should be considered. The first has to do with making accurate judgments about and providing useful feedback to interns. The second has to do with making judgments about how effectively the internship program is meeting its mission and goals. Each of these purposes requires that planners and evaluators be knowledgeable about and have the skill to employ a variety of evaluation methods.

This chapter focuses on these evaluation purposes. First, it summarizes what should be examined in the evaluation of interns' performances. Second, it summarizes what should be included in the evaluation of the internship program itself. Lastly, it presents an array of methodological approaches that can be used to obtain the information required for making judgments about interns and the internship program.

Evaluation is concerned with ten key dimensions (Nevo, 1983): (1) the definition of how evaluation will be employed; (2) its functions and (3) objectives; (4) pertinent information to be collected for each objective; (5) the criteria for judging merit; (6) who is to be served by the effort; (7) the processes to be employed; (8) the methods of inquiry to be used; (9) who should conduct the evaluation; and (10) the standards for judging the evaluation effort. These general issues should be considered when evaluating interns and internship programs.

EVALUATION OF INTERNS' PERFORMANCE

The major concern of evaluation is to provide supportive and corrective feedback that helps interns move through the program and prepares them

for their initial administrative positions. Here we discuss both the chronological stages at which evaluation should occur and the topical areas that are
of concern. The relationship of stages and topical areas can be depicted in a
matrix, as shown in Figure 7.1. Note, however, that this array should be
viewed as a general framework that is open to modification, according to
variations in mission, goals, and program design; readers are encouraged to
examine ways of adapting the matrix to fit their unique situations.

The Five Evaluation Stages

Evaluation should be both *formative* and *summative*. Formative evaluation, which helps to establish a baseline and provide early indicators of effectiveness so that modifications can be made as required, is the focus of the
first three stages. Summative evaluation, which is intended to provide a basis
for judgment about outcomes, is the focus of the last two stages.

Admissions to the Program. During the first stage the emphasis is on
identifying applicants' potential as interns and administrators. This diagnos-
tic information is vitally important, because it is needed to guide decisions
about who is admitted to the program and to design individualized professional development activities for those accepted. Appendix C includes a new
interns expectations survey that might be useful for designing purposes.

Early Clinical Experiences. The second stage is concerned with establishing the "game plan" for each intern. During this stage an academic course
of study is established and expectations for field experiences are developed.
These expectations should be listed in the contracts described in Chapter 5.
If this is done, the evaluation will follow naturally; that is, there will be a
standard of expectations by which to judge results in both the academic program and the field experience.

Midpoint Feedback. The third stage involves monitoring how well interns are performing in the contractually agreed-upon academic and field experiences. For academic performance in specific courses, timely completion
of projects and assignments and overall grade-point averages are of concern.
For field experiences, the quality of performance, adherence to contract expectations, and effectiveness of working relationships with site administrators
and field supervisors are all of interest.

Conclusion of the Program. The fourth part of the evaluation comes
when interns are about to move to their first administrative assignments. At
this point final judgment must be made concerning the extent to which each

FIGURE 7.1: Stages of Evaluation Needs

EVALUATION TOPICS	EVALUATION STAGES				
	Admission to Intern Programs	Early Clinical Experiences	Midpoint Feedback	Closing Stages of Program	Post-Program
Opportunities to self-select in/out of administration					
Potential as an administrator					
Career directions					
Professional growth needs					
Evidence of professional growth					
Internship activities/ contracting					
Mindset: Teaching to administration					
Resource use: People and materials					
Networking					
Readiness to enter job market					

intern has actually met initial expectations. These evaluations of academic performance and fieldwork inform recommendations for either continuing professional development or specific administrative positions applied for.

Postprogram. Finally, evaluation should focus on graduates' overall sense of growth in the program and their subsequent professional accomplishments (see Appendix C for a sample alumni evaluation form). Ultimately success must be measured according to their ability to move into administrative positions, perform well as educational leaders, and pursue leadership roles that fit with their career goals. In addition to knowing the extent to which learnings are applied by program graduates, this information should also be very helpful in the effort to monitor and change the program to assure its effectiveness.

Topical Areas to Be Evaluated

A major task is to ascertain *what* is to be evaluated regarding interns' performance at each of the stages. We have identified eleven topics (see Figure 7.1) that should be considered when evaluating interns' potential and performance and that are described in detail below. These eleven topics are not inclusive, but they should provide a solid basis for evaluation. They can also provide a basis for rectifying identified shortcoming at each of the evaluation stages.

Some topical areas, such as professional growth needs, are of interest in all the stages. Others, such as internship activities/contracting, are only of concern at specific stages. Those charged with evaluating interns' growth will want to determine what topical areas are to be evaluated at which programmatic stages.

Opportunities to Self-Select in/out of Administration. From initial inquiry about the program to completion and search for positions, interns should be encouraged to introspect about whether an administrative career is right for them. This should include consideration of their own perception of effectiveness and satisfaction in their preadministrative roles. It should also include opportunities to introspect regarding the administrative perspectives they have gained through the internship experience and how these experiences fit with initial expectations about administrative careers. Such opportunities should assist interns in making the best possible choices about professional career paths. It may lead some interns to conclude that administration is not what they had initially anticipated; others may conclude that they dislike or are ill fitted to play administrative roles.

Potential as an Administrator. To ensure that they are preparing superior leaders, the intern director and staff need feedback about interns' potential for careers in administration, as measured by ability, performance, and aptitude. This means making difficult judgments about candidates' potential as administrators at every stage of the program—including the possibility of counseling some individuals out of the program.

Career Directions. At the outset of the program, most interns will have a relatively limited notion of career possibilities. Most anticipate careers as vice-principals and principals. Perhaps because they come from school-based positions, that is the only administrative world they know. However, as noted in Chapter 6, there are many options available, both as first positions and as one's career develops over time. Therefore, it is important to regularly assess interns' performance and help them to ascertain the best fit between interests/strengths and career opportunities. As interns have opportunities to interact with various educational leaders who occupy different administrative roles, many will modify or expand upon their career expectations. This dynamic should be considered as an ongoing part of evaluation.

Professional Growth Needs. Each intern has a unique profile of experiences, knowledge, aptitudes, style of presentation, and personality. Therefore program staff must work with interns to construct relevant, individualized program experiences. This means developing an initial set of purposes, experiences to fulfill them, and periodic reviews of them at appropriate points in the program.

Evidence of Professional Growth. With agreement reached about what should be included in each intern's program, it is important to monitor progress and provide feedback about achievements. This is needed for support and encouragement. It is also important for midcourse modifications based upon evaluation of how well expectations are being achieved.

Internship Activities/Contracting. In earlier chapters we spoke of the importance of creating a meaningful set of learning experiences at the school site. The contract, which summarizes these expectations, should also serve as the basis for evaluating performance. Evaluation of interns' performance in the field is both formative and summative (i.e., it should provide corrective feedback and, ultimately, solid judgment about the intern's readiness and ability to perform effectively as an administrator).

Relationship with Site Administrator. As noted in Chapter 5, a positive working relationship between interns and site administrators is essential for interns to maximize opportunities to learn the craft of administration. This relationship should be monitored closely by field supervisors. Formative evaluations should be conducted so that decisions ranging from maintaining the status quo, to negotiating modifications in the relationship, to moving the intern to a different site situation, can be made. Appendix C includes a survey instrument to help establish the perceptions of site supervisors.

Mindset: Teaching to Administration.   Many candidates in administrative internship programs initially have rather unrealistic notions about what administrators do and how they think. Their previous professional roles do not provide opportunities to view the enterprise in the same way that administrators do. One of the purposes of the internship program should be to help interns gain a more realistic perspective about the role of administrators. This change in perspective is necessary so that interns can become knowledgeable about what is really required to perform efficiently and effectively as an administrator and so that they can make reasonable choices about whether they really want to fill such roles.

Use of Resources: People and Materials.   Much of administration has to do with locating and obtaining resources, both people and material, and then applying these resources to enhance educational effectiveness. As such, interns should have maximum opportunities to learn skills associated with these activities and the chance to apply them at their field sites. Evaluation of their effectiveness regarding resource utilization is essential when forming judgments about their potential as administrators.

Networking.   Chapter 6 explored networking as an activity that can help interns obtain administrative positions as well as assist them in forming support systems. Interns should be encouraged to develop and expand professional networks during their time in the program. During the course of the program, staff should evaluate how well they are progressing in developing such networks and provide feedback to ensure that their efforts are successful.

Readiness to Enter the Job Market

Interns will learn and develop at their own unique pace. At the conclusion of their preparation some may be ready to take on an administrative position, others may demonstrate need for further growth in specific areas, and still others some may show little evidence of readiness. The internship staff must make the best judgment possible of each intern's readiness. It is ethically important to provide honest and accurate feedback to interns themselves as well as to individuals who are considering hiring them for adminis-trative positions.

EXERCISE 7.1
A Matrix to Guide Intern Evaluation Efforts

The topical areas identified in Figure 7.1 cover major concerns that should be included in feedback and judgment regarding interns' performance and potential. Staff are encouraged to include discussion of the matrix at seminar sessions during all stages of the program, so that all participants understand the purpose and content that form the basis of interns' evalua-tions. Such sessions also provide opportunities to identify other topics which might be appropriate for particular situations.

Guiding questions for such discussions might include:

- Are the topical areas appropriate for the specific program and its in-terns?
- What additional topical areas might also be considered?
- During each of the five stages what specific information should be included for each of the topical areas?
- Who should be involved in planning, designing, and conducting the evaluations?
- When and where should feedback occur?
- What form should the evaluation feedback take?

EVALUATION OF THE INTERNSHIP PROGRAM

The second major evaluation concern has to do with maintaining, chang-ing, and improving the internship program. This is necessary both to ascer-tain whether the program is functioning as intended and to promote modi-fications if changes are needed for the program to remain viable. Figure 7.2 summarizes the program elements and the evaluation areas that need to be considered for each of these elements, all of which are described below.

Program Elements to be Evaluated

The program can be viewed as including six elements: recruitment, selec-tion, socialization, academic activities, clinical activities, and readiness for administration. Each element should be evaluated to assure that appropriate services are designed and delivered in the most effective way possible.

FIGURE 7.2: Program Elements and Evaluation Areas

EVALUATION AREAS	PROGRAM ELEMENTS							
	Recruitment	Selection	Socialization	Academic Activities	Clinical Activities			Readiness for Administration
					Supervision	Site Activities	Seminar	
Mission and Purposes								
Structures								
Processes								
Behaviors								
Adaptability								
Outcomes								

Recruitment. Recruitment should involve aggressive identification of potentially excellent administrators rather than reliance on those who, on their own initiative, decide to apply. The increasing demand for educational leaders rather than maintainers/managers requires that this search be monitored on a regular basis.

Selection. Selection processes, as noted in Chapter 2, are numerous. They include written statements, interviews, letters of recommendation, and, with increasing frequency, behaviorally anchored assessment centers. Making informed judgments about potential candidates depends on the extent to which these processes provide accurate and complete information. As such, they should be evaluated on a regular basis and modified as necessary.

Socialization. The major purpose of the program is to help interns perform as exemplary administrators. This is facilitated through a variety of program elements, including academic coursework, school-site activities, cohort development, networking, and the internship seminar. The changes in interns' sense of self are as important as the knowledge and skills attained. As such, the extent to which these changes occur should be evaluated.

Academic Activities. Virtually all preparation programs are required to evaluate academic activities on a regular basis. The demand for such audits comes from sources as diverse as internal university units, accrediting agencies, professional associations, and state education agencies. However, these demands are for general feedback concerning academic programs. What is also required is special emphasis on the effectiveness of the academic program as it relates to the needs of interns. For example, how well faculty members role model positive instructional leadership behaviors, their responsiveness to observations interns gain from their field assignments, and the applicability of course content to the practitioner's world should all be evaluated.

Clinical Activities. What is being evaluated here is the extent to which clinically related activities actually prepare interns as administrators. There are three distinct areas that should be evaluated: *clinical supervision,* which entails the effectiveness of field supervisors' and site administrators' abilities to provide growth experiences for interns; *site activities,* which should be based on the contracts and which are intended to help interns become competent as administrators; and the *internship seminar,* which should provide opportunities for further exploration and development of knowledge, skills, orientation, and attitudinal modification, as well as opportunities to process and better understand site-based observations and experiences.

Readiness for Administration.   Ultimately the effectiveness of the program must be measured against the extent to which it prepares interns to become administrators. Evaluation for this purpose should include information and judgments about the extent to which interns grow as potential administrators from entry to exit in the program; the number and percent of interns who are successful in obtaining administrative positions; how well they perform in these positions; and whether they are promoted into increasingly responsible positions. Measurement of outcomes against the outcomes obtained by similar institutions in the geographic region, as well as follow-up studies of program graduates, are strongly recommended.

Areas to be Evaluated

Each of these program elements should be evaluated according to six specific areas. As identified in Figure 7.2, these include mission and purposes, structures, processes, behaviors, adaptability, and outcomes.

Mission and Purposes.   This is the guiding force on which the entire effort should be based. Assuming that mission and purposes have been discussed, agreed upon, and put in writing, the extent to which they have been achieved can then be evaluated. That is, does the program do what it was intended to do?

Structures.   Structures, which should facilitate accomplishment of desired ends, have to do with the way the program is organized, who has what decisional responsibilities, the way communications flow, and how clear and accessible these structures are to those who need to employ them. Evaluation should include the extent to which these structures fit the purposes of the program and the degree to which they work.

Processes.   Processes established to make structures function effectively also need to be reviewed and modified as necessary. Processes include policy statements, rules, reporting procedures, and approaches to problem solving and decision making. Evaluation of written policies and procedures as well as observation of decision-making and problem-solving activities should form an important part of the overall evaluation effort.

Behaviors.   Behaviors that are exhibited by faculty and staff members are as important as the content of the program. Staff and faculty behaviors should be consonant with behaviors expected of interns. It is not enough to tell interns to "do as I say." Rather, staff and faculty must act as positive role models (i.e., "do as I do"). Thus staff and faculty behaviors should be examined to establish the extent to which they match program purposes and "model the way" for interns.

Adaptability. Given a rapidly changing environment, responsiveness and flexibility are important, so internship programs must show strong evidence of being adaptable. Evaluation should include information that has to do with these aspects of the program. Even the most carefully designed programs will soon be out of touch with the environment if efforts are not made to monitor achievements and make such changes as conditions require. In addition, internship programs must be responsive to the unique needs of individual interns and the situations they encounter at their work sites.

Outcomes. Finally, the continuation and future health of the program depends on results, which will determine whether the program prospers, barely scrapes by, or is abandoned. Criteria here include achievement of mission and purposes, placement of graduates, reputation, and continuing commitment on the part of all parties involved. Gathering information that can be used to judge whether these criteria are being satisfied is an absolute must in the program evaluation effort.

EXERCISE 7.2
Exploring the evaluation plan

Evaluation is best guided by involvement of faculty, staff, interns, and school district leaders who have a commitment to the program. Figure 7.2 might be discussed by a group representing all interested parties to identify the specific information to be obtained in each of the matrix cells. Questions similar to those suggested for guiding the evaluation of interns in Exercise 7.1 might also be useful for evaluation of the program:

- Are the categories suggested in Figure 7.2 appropriate for the program under review?
- Are there other categories that should also be addressed?
- What specific information should be sought to adequately evaluate each cell of the matrix?
- Who should be involved in the evaluation effort?
- How should the evaluation feedback be organized?
- When should evaluation feedback be ready for review, discussion, and decision making?

METHODOLOGICAL APPROACHES

Thus far this chapter has focused on the identification of *what* should be included in the evaluation of interns' performance and the internship program. In this final section we will explore alternative methodological approaches, or *how* necessary information can be obtained.

A full treatment of methodological considerations and techniques is well beyond the scope of the book. Readers who are interested in a detailed description of methodological strategies should turn to texts that focus on this topic (e.g., Backstrom & Hursh, 1963; Conway, Jennings, & Milstein, 1974; Fitz-Gibbon & Morris, 1987; Good, 1966; Likert, 1938; Parten, 1950; Richardson, Dowrehnwend, & Klein, 1965; Stecher & Davis, 1987). What follows are some general considerations that can help establish an overall approach to evaluation methods.

Two Guiding Criteria

Evaluation efforts should be guided by two important criteria. First, *multiple methods should be used to yield accurate and complete information.* Each methodological approach—document analysis, interviews, observations, and questionnaires—has particular strengths and weaknesses for yielding relevant information (see Figure 7.3). For example, it may be important to get perceptual feedback regarding how well site administrators think interns can write. This might best be done through interviews. However, if evaluators want to draw their own conclusions regarding interns' writing abilities, they may want to turn to document analysis of memos, newsletters, and other written materials that interns have drafted. The point is that "in general it is probable that several techniques employed in tandem will provide greater breadth and depth of information than will any single technique" (Conway, et al., 1974, p. 36). Often this use of multiple methods is referred to as "triangulation" (see Denzin, 1978; Jick, 1984).

Second, *information should be obtained as efficiently as possible.* Resources—including time, money, and skilled methodologists—are likely to be in limited supply. The maximum amount of information should be obtained with the lowest possible investment of energy, time, and money. For example, if a questionnaire is designed, it should be comprehensive, providing as much information as possible about the evaluation categories identified in Figures 7.1 and 7.2. The same holds true for interviews, observations, and document analysis.

FIGURE 7.3: Strengths and Weaknesses of Four Evaluation Methods

EVALUATION COMPONENTS

METHOD	Planning and Development	Adaptability and Flexibility	Time and Effort	Skill Required	Information Yield
Document Analysis	Simple: only requires identification of document sources	Very little: documents represent past events and situations	Very little: usually easy to collect, maintain, and retrieve	Moderate: if criteria are clear, training can be done with ease	Varies: depends on value of documents collected for analysis
Interviews	Relatively simple: appropriate questions must be identified	Extensive: the face-to-face interaction permits opportunities to probe and clarify	Very much: they consume much time both in gathering and in analyzing information	Very much: requires skill and experience to obtain, record, and analyze results	Extensive: can yield depth as well as serendipity due to opportunity to probe
Observations	Varies in difficulty: depends on accessibility	Varies: depends on how frequently observable events occur	Very much: requires being present at events and time to observe, record, and analyze	Very much: requires ability to sort out complex phenomena and to record fully and accurately	Extensive: provides opportunities to record actual behaviors
Questionnaires	Difficult to prepare: takes some time and should be reviewed for clarity, completeness, and reliability	Very little: respondents only interact with the written instrument	Very little: many responses can be collected and analyzed with little effort	Very much: construction is difficult and must be done well	Moderate: provides information from many individuals but is limited in depth of results

Choosing Methodologies

At least initially, evaluators will probably want to consider including document analysis, interviews, observations, and questionnaires as elements in their approach to evaluation. As Figure 7.3 indicates, each method can contribute to the evaluation effort in unique ways. Each also has advantages and disadvantages that should be taken into consideration when plans are made for evaluation efforts.

There are specific criteria that should be considered (Conway et al., 1974) when selecting methods for a particular information gathering need. Figure 7.4 displays the four methods presented above and the five criteria that should help guide the selection of methods to include in an evaluation. These criteria are described below.

Accessibility. Which method(s) is (are) likely to yield the desired information most readily? For example, acquiring the information needed to assess the behaviors of staff and faculty will probably require observations of these behaviors. When two or more methods are likely to yield similar results, the most economical one should be selected. In this case, both interviews and questionnaires can be used to ascertain opinions about the program, but the latter can result in a greater number of responses, probably with less effort.

FIGURE 7.4: Methods and Criteria for Selection

CRITERIA FOR SELECTING METHODS	METHODS			
	Document Analysis	Interviews	Observations	Questionnaires
Accessibility				
Relevance				
Accuracy				
Economy of Resources				
Skill and Time				

Relevance.   Beyond access, which method(s) is (are) likely to result in the development of useful and complete information that directly answers the questions posed? As an example, document analysis of brochures and other public relations–oriented documents is not as likely to establish how effectively program mission and purposes are being achieved as would interviews of interns, alumni, and those who have hired graduates of the program.

Accuracy.   Which method(s) has (have) the potential of producing the most precise and correct information? This question can only be answered as it relates to specific information requirements. For example, if the intent is to establish how selective admissions are, it may be more appropriate to refer to documents that record the ratio of applicants as compared with the number of candidates admitted to the program, than to interview students or others concerning their opinions about this topic.

Of course, confidence regarding accuracy may require that two or more methods be employed to get the information. Regarding the above example, evaluators may want to ascertain both the facts (i.e., what the documents tell them about selectivity) and the reputation (i.e., what interviews or questionnaires tell them about peoples' beliefs about selectivity).

Economy of Resources.   Which method(s) is (are) likely to produce the desired information in the most efficient manner? Economy has to do with time and energy consumed as well as fiscal inputs. As noted in Figure 7.3, document analysis and questionnaires are usually the most economical methods, and observations and interviews are the most expensive ones. If questionnaires are likely to yield the desired information as well as interviews will, then by all means use a questionnaire. Be careful, however, not to choose methods that may result in great economy but poor information.

Skill and Time.   How skilled are evaluators at using the different methodologies? In addition, do they have the time required to perform the necessary activities? It is not enough to select the most appropriate methodologies if skilled personnel are not available to conduct necessary activities. Similarly, if everyone is overburdened with other tasks, it is unlikely that sufficient time and attention will be given to evaluation activities. An honest assessment of these conditions should be made early in the effort to avoid undue frustration and to minimize pitfalls.

EXERCISE 7.3
Methods and criteria: Making the right choices

After identifying the information that is required, evaluators must make choices among several methodological alternatives available to them. Exercise 7.3 is intended to help in this effort. For this exercise it is recommended that:

- The evaluators should include interns, staff, faculty, and field leaders.
- The group should agree on the purposes of the evaluation. The more specific the purposes, the more likely it is that the group will be able to make good methodological decisions.
- Copies of Figure 7.4 should be reproduced in sufficient numbers so that each identified purpose can be explored on individual worksheets.
- After agreeing on a specific purpose, the group should discuss strengths and weaknesses of each of the four methods for that purpose. Each cell on Figure 7.4 should be filled in. A suggested typology to use for the discussion is:
  - *Poor:* The method will not meet the criteria very well
  - *Moderate:* The method will meet the criteria in some ways, but not in others
  - *Strong:* the method will lend itself well to the criteria
- The group should then review their responses and reach consensus about which method(s) should be employed.
- After repeating this exercise for each of the identified evaluation purposes, the group can then pool their decisions about methods and combine information requirements. For example, if three purposes call for the use of questionnaire development, items related to these purposes can be combined on a single instrument.

IN CONCLUSION

This chapter has been devoted to evaluation of interns' performance and program effectiveness. This important task must be attended to well and as an ongoing effort if one expects to know how things are going and what improvements are required.

Evaluation brings us full cycle. In effect, evaluation is based on the assumption that there will always be a need for renewal. The information we obtain through evaluation provides the basis for decision making about the future, both for continuing development of individual interns and program graduates, and for the modifications and changes that guarantee the continued integrity and relevance of the program itself.

Epilogue

THIS SECTION PROVIDES us with a final opportunity to highlight our perspective regarding internship programs. We hope that internship program planners and participants alike will agree with our perspective and seek to implement programs that reflect it.

The intent of the book is to provide suggestions that can promote the development and maintenance of outstanding internship programs. Properly employed, the book can coherently bring together the many aspects of preparation of tomorrow's educational leaders. These aspects include questions regarding who should participate, what the program design should be, what knowledge bases should be incorporated, how participants should relate to one another, how interns can make the transition from preparation to the administrative world, and the role of evaluation and ways that it can be conducted.

We live in difficult and exciting times that challenge us to respond in new and different ways. Education is confronted with a rapidly changing environment and a more global perspective, which have extraordinary implications for the way we structure and relate to one another in our schools as well as for how and what we teach in our curricula.

It follows that there are also implications for the way that we go about preparing educational leaders. It is not an exaggeration to say that our ability to provide meaningful experiences for tomorrow's educational leaders can have a profound effect on the future of education and, ultimately, on the health of our society in general.

We take it as a given that education will undergo significant changes over the next several decades. We *must* make every effort to assure that those who will be charged with making these changes happen will have the confidence, enthusiasm, skills, knowledge, and insights required to perform their roles well.

Our crystal ball is rather murky when it comes to education's future course. Because it is so murky, internship programs must be developed that are flexible and marked by innovativeness, creativity, and risk taking. They must be so both because the times call for extraordinary responses in our preparation of tomorrow's educational leaders and because those completing our internship programs must also be innovative, creative risk takers if they are going to be up to the challenges they will confront as tomorrow's educational leaders.

It is likely that internship programs will have to be constructed, reviewed, dismantled, rebuilt, and redesigned with frustrating regularity if they are to be effective. This is likely to be true for some time, because we are just beginning to explore ways of responding to the realities of the situation. There are many independent internship experiments going on across the country, including modifications of traditional university-based programs, partnership programs between universities and school districts, and a variety of consortia of universities, school districts, and state education agencies. As the results of these experiments are disseminated, we will need to review them and derive lessons for our particular program efforts.

Perhaps there was not the same sense of urgency about examining how and how well educational leaders were prepared in the past as there is today. Certainly the demonstrated demands for significant improvement of preparation of tomorrow's educational leaders are great. Whatever the future holds, we believe it will not provide the luxury of responding as we have in the past. Criticisms of preparation of educational leaders abound. It will only get worse in the future if we do not now take the initiative that is so clearly required.

To live in interesting times is both a special gift and a heavy responsibility. May we be up to the challenge.

APPENDIXES

REFERENCES

INDEX

ABOUT THE AUTHOR

FIGURE A.1: Checklist for Mentoring Skills

MENTORING SKILLS: A SELF-ASSESSMENT

For each of the following skills, please circle the number that best describes your present degree of comfort.

| | DEGREE OF COMFORT | | | |
SKILL	Highly Un-comfortable	Uncom-fortable	Somewhat Un-comfortable	Most Com-fortable
A. Carrying out the helping relationship	1	2	3	4
B. Matching helping style to maturity level of another	1	2	3	4
C. Modeling conflict-resolution behaviors	1	2	3	4
D. Working through the problem-solving process with another	1	2	3	4
E. Coaching another after observation	1	2	3	4

HELPING RELATIONSHIP CHECKLIST

	Yes	No
A. Overall Assessment		
1. Was my client able to identify the problem?	___	___
2. Was my client able to identify the direction he/she wanted to go?	___	___
3. Was my client, having taken steps 1 and 2 above, able to decide on a direction he/she was going to take in addressing the problem?	___	___
B. My behavior		
1. Did I consciously try to hear each word my client expressed?	___	___
2. Did I look my client in the eye as he/she was relating concerns?	___	___
3. Did I knowingly behave in a directive or nondirective way during the conference?	___	___
4. Can I support my response to (3) with data?	___	___
5. Did I try to paraphrase or check out my perceptions during the conference?	___	___
6. Did I try to help my client become more responsible for his/her behavior?	___	___
C. Client Behavior		
1. Did my client come close to or select a problem-solving strategy?	___	___
2. Can I support my response to (1) with data?	___	___
3. Did my client feel positively about himself/herself at the close of the conference?	___	___
4. Was my client able to summarize accurately the outcomes of the conference?	___	___

Source: J. Daresh & M. Playko. (1989). *Administrative Mentoring: A Training Manual.* Columbus, OH: The Ohio LEAD Center. Reproduced by permission.

APPENDIX A:

Guidelines

MENTORING

Desired Characteristics of Mentors

The following list of characteristics may assist in the selection of site administrators who have the potential for mentoring.

1. Demonstrated desire to help others extend present levels of performance and aspiration.
2. Consistent modeling of the principles of life-long learning.
3. Ability to question as well as offer suggestions.
4. Demonstrated positive leadership qualities such as:
    A. Intelligence
    B. Effective oral and written communication skills
    C. Acceptance of alternative solutions to complex problems
    D. Vision and the ability to communicate that vision
    E. Well-established interpersonal skills
5. Awareness of the political and social realities of the enterprise.

Functions of Mentoring

The veteran administrator who acts as a mentor to interns must perform a number of functions, which are listed below (Daresh & Playko, 1989; Wasden & Muse, 1987). Administrators can be aided in evaluating their own performance in these areas by using the self-assessment checklist shown in Figure A.1.

1. *Advising:* Responds to the intern's requests for information in a timely and effective manner
2. *Appraising:* Formally and informally evaluates the intern throughout the internship
3. *Coaching:* Demonstrates the skills of effective job performance and pro-

vides the intern opportunities to practice those skills in nonthreatening situations

4. *Communicating:* Maintains open lines of communication with the intern and actively listens to the intern's concerns
5. *Counseling:* Provides empathetic emotional support and personal and professional assistance to the intern
6. *Guiding:* Orients the intern to the unwritten rules, norms, and culture of administration and the organization
7. *Modeling:* Displays attributes and behaviors that exhibit professionalism and patterns for the intern to follow
8. *Motivating:* Encourages pursuit of goals the intern has set
9. *Protecting:* Serves as a buffer by providing a safe environment where mistakes can be made without posing danger and risking self-confidence
10. *Developing skills:* Helps the intern learn the skills of administration and instructional leadership at gradually increasing levels of complexity
11. *Sponsoring:* Uses influence in the district or agency to advance the intern's career through information and recommendations
12. *Supervising:* Delegates to the intern, with subsequent feedback, analysis, and dialogue
13. *Teaching:* Instructs the intern in the specific skills and knowledge necessary for successful performance
14. *Validating:* Evaluates, modifies, and endorses the intern's performance, goals, and aspirations

Selected Bibliography on Mentoring

Alleman, E., Cochran, J., Doverspike, J., & Newman, I. (1984). Enriching mentoring relationships. *The Personnel and Guidance Journal, 62,* 329–332.

Anderson, D. (1982). *Toward a theory of stewardship: A stewardship primer.* Provo, UT: Brigham Young University.

Anderson, E., & Shannon, A. (1988). Leadership: Toward a conceptualization of mentoring. *Journal of Teacher Education, 1,* 38–42.

Bova, B., & Phillips, R. (1984). Mentoring as a learning experience for adults. *Journal of Teacher Education, 35*(3), 16–20.

Clawson, J. (1985). Is mentoring necessary? *Training and Development Journal, 39*(4), 36–39.

Collins, E., & Scott, P. (1978). Everyone who makes it has a mentor. *Harvard Business Review, 56*(4), 89–101.

Daresh, J., & Playko, M. (1989). *Administrative mentoring: A training manual.* Columbus, OH: The Ohio LEAD Center.

Galvez-Hjornevik, C. (1986). Mentoring among teachers: A review of the literature. *Journal of Teacher Education, 37*(1), 6–11.

Gehrke, J. (1988). On preserving the essence of mentoring as one form of teacher leadership. *Journal of Teacher Education, 1*(1), 43–45.

Gerstein, M. (1985). Mentoring: An age old practice in knowledge-based society. *Journal of Counseling and Development, 64*(2), 156–157.

Gray, W., & Gray, M. (1985). Synthesis of research on mentoring beginning teachers. *Educational Leadership, 43*(3), 37–43.

Gray, W., & Gray, M. (1986). *Mentoring: Aid to excellence in education, the family, and the community.* Vancouver, British Columbia: Xerox Reproduction Centre.

Hennecke, M. (1983). Mentors and proteges: How to build relationships that work. *Training, 20*(7), 36–41.

Hurley, D. (1988). The mentor mystique. *Psychology Today, 22*(5), 41–43.

Johnson, M. (1980). Mentors—the key to development and growth. *Training and Development Journal, 34*(7), 55–57.

Krupp, J. (1985). Mentoring: A means of sparking school personnel. *Journal of Counseling and Development, 64*(2), 154–155.

Lea, D., & Leibowitz, Z. (1983). Mentors: Would you know one if you saw one? *Supervisory Management, 28*(4), 33–35.

Merriam, S. (1983). Mentors and proteges: A critical review of the literature. *Adult Education Quarterly, 33*(3), 161–173.

Phillips-Jones, L. (1982). *Mentors and proteges.* New York: Arbor House.

Phillips-Jones, L. (1983). Establishing a formalized mentoring program. *Training and Development Journal, 37*(2), 38–43.

Roche, G. (1979). Much ado about mentors. *Harvard Business Review, 57*(3), 14–28.

Schmidt, J., & Wolfe, J. (1980). The mentor partnership: Discovery of professionalism. *NASPA Journal, 17*(3), 45–51.

Taylor, S. (1986). Mentors: Who are they and what are they doing? *Thrust for Educational Leadership 15*(6), 39–41.

Wasden, D., & Muse, I. (1987). *The mentoring handbook.* Provo, UT: Brigham Young University.

Zey, M. (1984). *The mentor connection.* Homewood, IL: Dow Jones-Irwin.

PROBLEM PROJECT DEVELOPMENT

The following are suggested as areas to explore in developing the problem project. The intent is to examine the process from inception through evaluation.

1. *Trigger event(s):* How was the need determined?
2. *Nature and background of the problem:* How was the problem defined? In what knowledge base is the problem founded? What research supports that knowledge base? The intern should consult as much research as possible relative to the problem project. Information from a research base includes support for (1) the rationale of the project, (2) the definition of the problem, (3) its planning, (4) development, (5) implementation, and (6) evaluation.

3. *Goals and objectives:* What is it the intern hopes to accomplish? Present in a list format.
4. *Plan of action:* What planning process was used? How was the problem-solving process developed? What progressive steps are likely to be involved in the project? Include proposed timelines and proposed deadlines. What evaluation measures will be used to determine the project's success?
5. *Development:* How did the problem project develop? Who was involved? How was participation gathered? Discuss the who/what/when/where/how/why of the project. How was the implementation process carried through? What are/were the methods for follow-up?
6. *Actual target dates:* Since the final write-up of the problem project may be due prior to the actual completion of the project, the paper should include target dates for specific activities that are not yet completed at the time of the write-up.
7. *Evaluation:* Describe the evaluation measures used to determine whether the problem project "made a difference." What objective data were gathered? What do the evaluation data suggest for future problem projects?

Professional Associations and Departments of Education

SOURCES FOR ADMINISTRATIVE COMPETENCY EXPECTATIONS

American Association of School Administrators
1801 North Moor Street
Arlington, VA 22209

Council of Chief State School Officers
Hall of the States, Suite 379
400 North Capitol Street, N.W.
Washington, DC 20001

National Association of Elementary
    School Principals
1615 Duke Street
Alexandria, VA 22314

National Middle School Association
4807 Evanswood Drive
Columbus, OH 43229

National Association of Secondary
    School Principals
1904 Association Drive
Reston, VA 22091

The Ohio L.E.A.D. Center
623-H Park Meadow Road
Westerville, OH 43081

STATE DEPARTMENTS OF EDUCATION

ALABAMA

Superintendent of Education
State Department of Education
501 Dexter Avenue
481 State Office Building
Montgomery, AL 36130
Telephone: (205) 261–5156

ALASKA

Commissioner of Education
State Department of Education
Pouch F
801 Juneau, AK 99811–9951
Telephone: (907) 465–2800

AMERICAN SAMOA

Director of Education
Department of Education
Pago Pago, Tutuila 96799
Telephone: (684) 633–5159

ARIZONA

Superintendent of Public Education
State Department of Education
1535 West Jefferson
Phoenix, AZ 85007
Telephone: (602) 542–4361

ARKANSAS

Director, General Education Division
State Department of Education
#4 Capitol Mail
Little Rock, AR 72201
Telephone: (501) 682–4475

CALIFORNIA

Superintendent of Public Instruction
State Department of Education
721 Capitol Hill
Sacramento, CA 94244–2720
Telephone: (916) 445–4338

COLORADO

Commisioner of Education
State Department of Education
201 East Colfax Avenue
Denver, CO 80203–1705
Telephone: (303) 866–6806

CONNECTICUT

Commissioner of Education
State Department of Education
165 Capitol Avenue
State Office Building, Room 308
Hartford, CT 06106
Telephone: (203) 566–5061

DELAWARE

Superintendent of Public Instruction
State Department of Education
P.O. Box 1402
Townsend Building 11279
Dover, DE 19903
Telephone: (302) 736–4601

DISTRICT OF COLUMBIA

Superintendent of Public Schools
District of Columbia Public Schools
415 Twelfth Street NW
Washington, DC 20004
Telephone: (202) 724–4222

FLORIDA

Commissioner of Education
State Department of Education

Capitol Building, Room PL 116
Tallahassee, FL 32399
Telephone: (904) 487–1785

GEORGIA

Superintendent of Schools
State Department of Education
2066 Twin Towers East
Capitol Square
Atlanta, GA 30334–5020
Telephone: (404) 656–2800

GUAM

Superintendent of Education
Department of Education
P.O. Box DE
Agana, Guam 96910
Telephone: (671) 472–8901

HAWAII

Superintendent of Schools
State Department of Education
P.O. Box 2360
1390 Miller Street, H307
Honolulu, HI 96804
Telephone: (808) 548–6405

IDAHO

Superintendent of Public Instruction
State Department of Education
650 West State Street
Boise, ID 83720
Telephone: (208) 334–3301

ILLINOIS

Interim Superintendent of Education
State Board of Education
100 North First Street
Springfield, IL 62777
Telephone: (217) 782–2221

INDIANA

Superintendent of Public Instruction
State Department of Education
State House, Room 229
100 North Capitol Street

Indianapolis, IN 46204–2798
Telephone: (317) 232–6612

IOWA

Director of Education
State Department of Education
Grimes State Office Building
East 14th and Grant Streets
Des Moines, IA 50319–0146
Telephone: (515) 281–5294

KANSAS

Commissioner of Education
State Department of Education
120 East 10th Street
Topeka, Kansas 66612
Telephone: (913) 296–3201

KENTUCKY

Superintendent of Public Instruction
State Department of Education
1725 Capitol Plaza Tower
Frankfort, KY 40601
Telephone (502) 564–4770

LOUISIANA

Superintendent of Education
State Department of Education
P.O. Box 94064
626 North 4th Street
Baton Rouge, LA 70804–9064
Telephone: (504) 342–3602

MAINE

Commissioner of Education
Department of Educational and Cul-
    tural Services
State House Station No. 23
Augusta, ME 04333
Telephone: (207) 289–5800

MARYLAND

State Superintendent of Schools
State Department of Education
200 West Baltimore Street
Baltimore, Maryland 21201
Telephone: (301) 333–2200

MASSACHUSETTS

Commissioner of Education
State Department of Education
Quincy Center Plaza
1385 Hancock Street
Quincy, MA 02169
Telephone: (617) 770–7300

MICHIGAN

Superintendent of Public Instruction
State Department of Education
P.O. Box 30008
608 West Allegan Street
Lansing, Michigan 48909
Telephone: (517) 373–3354

MINNESOTA

Commissioner of Education
State Department of Education
712 Capitol Square Building
550 Cedar Street
St. Paul, MN 55101
Telephone: (612) 296–2358

MISSISSIPPI

Superintendent of Education
State Department of Education
P.O. Box 771
High Street
Jackson, MS 39205–0771
Telephone: (601) 359–3513

MISSOURI

Commissioner of Education
State Department of Elementary/Sec-
    ondary Education
P.O. Box 480
Jefferson State Office Building
205 Jefferson St., 6th Floor
Jefferson City, MO 65102
Telephone: (314) 751–4446

MONTANA

Superintendent of Public Instruction
State Office of Public Instruction
106 State Capitol

Helena, MT 59620
Telephone: (406) 444–3654

NEBRASKA

Commissioner of Education
State Department of Education
P.O. Box 94987
301 Centennial Mall, South
Lincoln, NE 68509
Telephone: (402) 471–2465

NEVADA

Superintendent of Public Instruction
State Department of Education
400 West King Street
Capitol Complex
Carson City, NV 89710
Telephone: (720) 885–3301

NEW HAMPSHIRE

Commissioner of Education
State Department of Education
101 Pleasant Street
State Office Park South
Concord, NH 03301
Telephone: (603) 271–4144

NEW JERSEY

Commissioner of Education
State Department of Education
225 West State Street
Trenton, NJ 08625
Telephone: (609) 292–4450

NEW MEXICO

Superintendent of Public Instruction
State Department of Education
Education Building
300 Don Gaspar
Santa Fe, NM 87501–2786
Telephone: (505) 827–6516

NEW YORK

Commissioner of Education
State Education Department

111 Education Building
Washington Avenue
Albany, NY 12234
Telephone: (581) 474–5844

NORTH CAROLINA

Superintendent of Public Instruction
State Department of Public Instruction
Education Building, Room 318
Edenton and Salisbury Streets
Raleigh, NC 27603–1712
Telephone: (919) 733–3813

NORTH DAKOTA

Superintendent of Public Instruction
State Department of Public Instruction
State Capitol Building, 11th Floor
600 Boulevard Avenue East
Bismarck, ND 58505–0164
Telephone (701) 224–2261

NORTH MARIANA ISLANDS

Superintendent of Education
Commonwealth of the Northern Mariana Islands
Department of Education
Saipan, CM 96950
Telephone: (670) 933–9812

OHIO

Superintendent of Public Instruction
State Department of Education
65 South Front Street
Room 808
Columbus, OH 43266–0308
Telephone: (614) 466–3304

OKLAHOMA

Superintendent of Public Instruction
State Department of Education
Oliver Hodge Memorial Education
   Building
2500 North Lincoln Boulevard
Oklahoma City, OK 73105–4599
Telephone: (405) 521–3301

OREGON

Superintendent of Public Instruction
State Department of Education
700 Pringle Parkway SE
Salem, OR 97310
Telephone: (503) 378–3573

PENNSYLVANIA

Interim Secretary of Education
State Department of Education
333 Market Street, 10th Floor
Harrisburg, PA 17126–0333
Telephone: (717) 787–5820

RHODE ISLAND

Commissioner of Education
State Department of Education
22 Hayes Street
Providence, RI 02908
Telephone: (401) 277–2031

SOUTH CAROLINA

Superintendent of Education
State Department of Education
1006 Rutledge Building
Columbia, SC 29201
Telephone: (803) 734–8492

SOUTH DAKOTA

Superintendent of Public Instruction
State Department of Education
Division of Elementary/Secondary
 Education
700 Governors Drive
Pierre, SD 57501
Telephone: (605) 773–3243

TENNESSEE   ,

Commissioner of Education
State Department of Education
100 Cordell Hull Building
Nashville, TN 37219
Telephone: (615) 741–2731

TEXAS

Commissioner of Education
Texas Education Agency
William B. Travis Building
1701 North Congress Avenue
Austin TX 78701
Telephone: (512) 463–8985

UTAH

Superintendent of Public Instruction
State Office of Education
250 East 50 South
Salt Lake City, UT 84111
Telephone: (801) 538–7500

VERMONT

Commissioner of Education
State Department of Education
120 State Street
Montpelier, VT 05602
Telphone: (802) 828–3135

VIRGINIA

Superintendent of Public Instruction
State Department of Education
P.O. Box 60—James Monroe Building
Fourteenth & Franklin Streets
Richmond, VA 23216–2060
Telephone: (804) 225–2023

WASHINGTON

Superintendent of Public Instruction
State Department of Public Instruction
Old Capitol Building
Washington & Legion
Mail Stop FG-11
Olympia, WA 98504
Telephone: (206) 586–6904

WEST VIRGINIA

State Superintendent of Schools
State Department of Education
Building B Room 358
1900 Washington Street
Charleston, WV 25305
Telephone: (304) 348–3644

WISCONSIN
Superintendent of Public Instruction
State Department of Education
125 South Webster Street
P.O. Box 7841
Madison, WI 53707
Telephone: (608) 266–1771

WYOMING
State Department of Public Instruction
State Department of Education
Hathaway Building
Cheyenne, WY 82002
Telephone: (307) 777–7675

DANFORTH PROGRAMS FOR THE PREPARATION OF PRINCIPALS

The Danforth Foundation-supported programs can serve as models for others who are developing innovative programs to prepare school administrators. Brochures and other materials can be obtained through the program facilitators. Other information may be obtained through the Danforth Office:

Danforth Foundation
231 South Bemiston Avenue
St Louis, MO 63105–1903

Area of Administration and Educational Leadership
University of Alabama
College of Education
Box Q
Tuscaloosa, AL 35487

School of Education and Human Development
California State University–Fresno
Department of Advanced Studies
Fresno, CA 93704–0003

Department of Administration, Rehabilitation, and Postsecondary Education
College of Education
San Diego State University
San Diego, CA 92182

Department of Educational Leadership
University of Connecticut
U 93
249 Glenbrook Road
Storrs, CT 06268

Educational Administration
University of Central Florida
144 Education Building
Orlando, FL 32816

Department of Educational Administration
Georgia State University
University Plaza
Atlanta, GA 30303

School of Education
Indiana University
902 West New York Street
Indianapolis, IN 46223

College of Education
Iowa State University
N229 Lagomarcino
Ames, IA 50011

Department of Educational Leadership
Western Kentucky University
Tate Page Hall 423 A
Bowling Green, KY 42101

School of Education
University of Massachusetts
210 Furcolo Hall
Amherst, MA 01003

Department of Educational Administration
College of Education
The University of New Mexico
Albuquerque, NM 87131

Director, City College Principals' Center
The City College of the City University of New York
Covenant Avenue at 138th Street
New York, NY 10031

College of Education
The Ohio State University
127 Arps Hall
1945 North High Street
Columbus, OH 43210

College of Education
University of Oklahoma
820 Van Vleet Oval
Norman, OK 73019

Department of Educational Administration
East Tennessee State University
Box 19000A
Johnson City, TN 37614

Department of Educational Leadership
The University of Tennessee–Knoxville
235 Claxton Addition
Knoxville, TN 67996

College of Education
University of Houston
4800 Calhoun Road
Houston, TX 77004

Department of Educational Leadership
Brigham Young University
310 MCKB
Provo, UT 84602

Department of Educational Leadership and Services
Old Dominion University
Norfolk, VA 23529

Department of Educational Leadership
College of Education
Virginia Tech
226 University City Office Building
Blacksburg, VA 24061

Department of Educational Leadership and Policy Studies
Ruffner Hall
University of Virginia
405 Emmet Street
Charlottesville, VA 22930

College of Education
University of Washington
M219 Miller Hall, DQ-12
Seattle, WA 98195

NATIONAL GROUPS AND ORGANIZATIONS WITH WHICH INTERNS SHOULD BE FAMILIAR

American Association of School Administrators
1801 North Moore Street
Arlington, VA 22209
Major publication—*The School Administrator*
Conference/convention—Februrary or March

American Educational Research Association
1230 Seventeenth Street, N.W.
Washington, D.C. 20036
Major publication—Multiple, dependent on interest and choice of affiliation
Conference/convention—March or April

Association for Supervision and Curriculum Development
1250 N. Pitt St.
Alexandria, VA 22314
Major publication—*Educational Leadership*
Conference/convention—February or March

National Association of Elementary School Principals
1615 Duke Street
Alexandria, VA 22314
Major publication—*Elementary Principal*
Conference/convention—March

National Association of Secondary School Principals
1904 Association Drive
Reston, VA 22091
Major Publication—*NASSP Journal*
Conference/convention—February

National Conference of Professors in Educational Administration
Department of Educational Administration
University of Wisconsin—Madison
Madison, WI 53706
Conference/convention—August

National Middle School Association
4807 Evanswood Drive
Columbus, OH 43229–6292
Major publication—*Middle School Journal*
Conference/convention—November

University Council for Educational Administration
Rackley Building
Pennsylvania State University
University Park, PA 16802
Major publication—*UCEA Review*
Conference/convention—October

APPENDIX C

Suggested Surveys and Evaluation Forms

NEW INTERNS' EXPECTATIONS SURVEY

Please answer the following questions as fully as you can. The information you provide will help us as we try to provide you with the best possible preparation program.

1. Why did you decide to apply for the program?
2. What are your expectations regarding field experiences in the program?
3. What are your expectations regarding academic experiences in the program?
4. What are your expectations regarding professional development in the program?
5. What do you anticipate, as regards time and effort, that will be required of you in the program?
6. Assuming that you have been thinking about the program, can you describe what you anticipate your experience will be like? Please draw as vivid a picture of that experience as you can.
7. Knowing yourself, how difficult do you think the program will be? Please be specific about the kinds of difficulties you anticipate.
8. You will be interacting with many people during the program. How intense do you anticipate your interactions will be with (Please circle appropriate responses):

	Low	Moderate	High
Other interns	*	*	*
Intern staff	*	*	*
Site supervisors	*	*	*
Educational Administration faculty	*	*	*

9. Are you interested in obtaining an administrative position?
____Yes____No.

If yes:

___Immediately following the program

___Within a year or so

___Sometime in the future

10. If you are seeking an administrative position, can you specify the role(s)?
11. If you are seeking an administrative position, to what extent will your participation in the program help you to obtain that position?

SURVEY OF SITE ADMINISTRATORS WHO HAVE SUPERVISED INTERNS

1. In what ways did the intern staff help prepare you for your role as an intern supervisor?
2. Are there other things you would recommend that the staff should do to help prepare site administrators for their roles as intern supervisors?
3. Was your relationship with field supervisors made clear to you? If so, how would you describe that relationship?
4. Could that relationship be improved in any way for the benefit of the intern? If so, how?
5. Did you and your intern develop a clear set of expectations regarding the activities that were to be included in the experience? If so, were these expectations delineated in the form of a contract?
6. If a contract was developed, did you find it to be useful? If so, how? If not, why not?
7. Did the intern shadow you, especially in the first part of his/her experience? If so, did you and the intern find this to be a useful exercise?
8. What activities were particularly helpful for your intern?
9. What activities did not prove to be very helpful for your intern?
10. Did you participate in the evaluation of your intern? If so, what was your role?
11. In your opinion, what are the greatest benefits of the field experience for the intern?
12. What intrinsic rewards do you get from being an intern site supervisor?
13. Are there other rewards that you think should be provided for site supervisors? If so, please specify.
14. Would you like to have more opportunities to meet with other site supervisors? If so, about how frequently and what would you like to have happen at such meetings?
15. Would you be willing to be a site supervisor again? Why/why not?
16. Do you have any specific suggestions for improving the program? We are particularly interested in any thoughts you may have about the field experience and the role of the site supervisor.

17. Is there anything else you think that the staff should be considering as it evaluates its efforts?

Please check the appropriate space:

    I am an

    ____Elementary principal

    ____Middle school principal

    ____High school principal

    ____Central office administrator

    ____Other:_____

ALUMNI EVALUATION OF INTERNSHIP/PROGRAM/PLACEMENT

It is important for the Educational Administration Department to hear from educators who have completed the internship program. Our ability to enhance and improve the program is dependent on your feedback. Please help us by taking the time to think about and complete this evaluation form.

I. Program Content

1. From the course list below, please rate those courses that you have taken as part of the program:

Course #	Course Title	Not Useful			Very Useful
_____	_____	1	2	3	4
_____	_____	1	2	3	4
_____	_____	1	2	3	4

(list all courses)

2. Which courses have you found most useful in preparing you for an administrative position?

    _____

    _____

    _____

3. Are there any specific courses you would delete from or add to the program of studies?

Delete	*Add*
_____	_____
_____	_____
_____	_____

4. What was the focus of your "problem" project (please check the category that is most descriptive)
_____Administrative policies/procedures/structures
_____Communications
_____Curriculum development
_____School/community
_____Teacher morale/school climate
_____Other (please specify)_____
5. How would you rate the problem project as a learning experience in relation to other field activities?
   Poor   1   2   3   4   Excellent
6. How would you rate the problem project as a learning experience with regard to a sense of leadership, change, and planning?
   Poor   1   2   3   4   Excellent
7. How would you rate the following aspects of the program?
   Scale: W   =   Weak aspect
          A   =   Acceptable aspect
          S   =   Strong aspect
   _____Academic coursework
   _____Campus-based supervisors' input
   _____Site-based administrator's input
   _____Internship seminars
   _____Problems exercise
   _____Other (please specify)_____
8. To what extent did you find the following to be problematic during the program?

	Not a problem			A major problem
Adding new roles	1	2	3	4
Time frame of the program	1	2	3	4
Site administrator's expectations	1	2	3	4
Home/personal responsibilities	1	2	3	4
Number of courses included in the program	1	2	3	4
Professors' course expectations	1	2	3	4
Travel expectations	1	2	3	4
Other: (_____)	1	2	3	4

II. *Networking and Cohort Development*

9. Did you find that your fellow interns were helpful to you in dealing with the intensity of the internship experience?
    ____Very helpful
    ____Somewhat helpful
    ____Not very helpful
10. If you answered "very helpful" or "somewhat helpful," in what ways were they helpful (check applicable responses):
    ____As listeners
    ____As idea givers
    ____As encouragers
    ____Other (please specify_____)
11. Have you maintained contact with other interns?
    ____Yes   ____No
12. If you maintain contact, with how many?_____
13. Approximately how frequently do you interact?
    ____Daily
    ____On average, weekly
    ____On average, monthly
    ____Other (please specify_____)
14. What is the nature of your continuing interactions?
    ____Mainly social
    ____Mainly professional
    ____Other (please specify_____)

III. *Status Regarding An Administrative Position*

15. Have you applied for an administrative position?
    ____Yes   ____No
16. If you sought an administrative position, when did you first do so?
    ____Immediately after the program
    ____A year after the program
    ____Other (please specify_____)
17. If you sought a position, were you successful?
    ____Yes   ____No
18. If you were successful, what is your role?
    ____Assistant principal
    ____Principal
    ____Program director/coordinator
    ____Activities director
    ____Other (please specify_____)

19. If you have not yet obtained an administrative position, how much time are you willing to devote to obtaining such a position?

    ____None; I've decided I don't want to do so

    ____None; I don't believe I can obtain one

    ____For another year or two

    ____Five years maximum

    ____Until I get one

    ____Other (please specify_____)

IV. Personal Issues

20. Was there a financial loss during the program?

    ____Yes____No.

    If so, was it a significant sacrifice for you?

    ____Extensive

    ____Somewhat

    ____Not much

21. Regarding your own development *as a person,* did the program have an impact?

    Hardly at all   1   2   3   4   Significantly

22. Did you find that you had a good support network to help you get through the program?

    ____Yes   ____No

23. Who formed the most important foundations of your support network?

	Not important			Very important
Intern staff	1	2	3	4
Colleagues at school/agency	1	2	3	4
Other interns	1	2	3	4
Friends	1	2	3	4
Significant others	1	2	3	4
Other (_____)	1	2	3	4

V. Outcome

24. Overall, how would you rate the program?

    Not worth the effort   1   2   3   4   Highly worthwhile

25. Would you do it over again, knowing what you know now?

    ____Yes   ____No

26. Give us your best shot: What else should we know that will help us be sensitive about program participants' needs and ways the program can be changed to be more responsive to those needs?

Brief Scenarios

The scenarios in Appendix D are provided for possible inclusion as a learning device in the internship seminar. They should facilitate lively interaction among interns around topics that are relevant to their professional development. The scenarios are focused on issues that are likely to be encountered (1) initially, (2) at the intermediate point, and (3) at more advanced stages in the program. Readers are encouraged to develop their own scenarios to encompass situationally based issues.

THE INITIAL STAGE

Scenario 1: How Did I Get into This?

Congratulations! You made it through the difficult screening process and you are in the internship program. You've registered for your first semester of classes and have carefully mapped out the things you will have to accomplish during the time that you will be in the program.

The reality of what you have committed yourself to has begun to sink in. Will you be able to do it all? Are you going to be able to meet the challenges involved? You know you have to confront such issues if you are going to come to peace with yourself.

Questions:
1. What are you feeling right now?
2. How will you come to grips with your concerns about your abilities to perform well as an intern?
3. What will you have to do if you expect to carry out your goals and objectives?

Scenario 2: I Wonder if I Can Do It All?

You began your internship program this month. You have not begun working in your school as an administrative intern yet, but you are beginning to become oriented to the school district and the university coursework. The feelings you are experiencing range from excitement about your ideas and how you will apply them at the school in which you will be working, to absolute fear of failure. You feel good about your cohort group. When you are together you have the feeling that anything is possible, but you still wonder whether you are going to be able to succeed in this program.

Questions:
1. What can you do about your emotional swings?
2. What are some of the factors that must be considered when thinking about whether you will succeed in the program?
3. How can your fellow interns help?

Scenario 3: Who Am I, Anyway?

Fall has arrived and your internship is just beginning. You have helped with registration, teacher orientation, last-minute room arrangements, faculty book orders, and parents who are asking for special consideration for their children. In the process you are surprised to find that you are experiencing a change in the way you think. Your perspective about the school is beginning to be less like that of many of your teacher friends and more like that of the principal.

Questions:
1. What is going on?
2. Will you be able to maintain your relationship with your teacher friends if this shift in thinking continues and maybe even increases?
3. Do you feel required to support your site administrator's views and positions?

Scenario 4: Am I Doing Anything Well?

There is just too much to do! You want to learn everything you can about administration, but you are finding it a bit bewildering. There is so much to be done, and there are not enough hours in the day. You are deeply concerned that you are not performing up to your normal high standards. You think that you are cutting corners and just keeping your head above water with the assignments your site supervisor has given you.

Questions:
1. How do you deal with the attitude that everything you do should be done very well?
2. How can you balance your many duties more satisfactorily?

THE INTERMEDIATE STAGE

Scenario 1: Community Involvement and Reticent Faculty

You began as an administrative intern in September. It is now November. Your administrative experiences have gradually evolved from "shadowing" your site administrator to expectations of increased administrative responsibility. You have been asked to work on school-community relations as part of your responsibilities. The faculty and staff at your school have previously been unresponsive to community needs and interests and have generally functioned in a provincial manner. They have indicated that they do not believe that the community is able or willing to contribute to the school. They have been known to make statements such as, "Oh, we tried that before" and "The parents don't seem to care."

Questions:
1. What is the problem as you see it from your perspective?
2. What strategies might you employ in order to successfully fulfill your site administrator's expectations?
3. What alternatives are available to you for enhancing the level and quality of involvement by the faculty and staff?

Scenario 2: Taking a Stance

You have just begun an internship experience at your home school. You have completed a summer session of coursework and have been actively involved in the opening of school activities. You have a clear understanding as to the nature and responsibilities of an administrative intern. During October, the lack of successful contract negotiations between the district's administration and the teachers' union has led to the possibility of a teachers' strike. You have been asked by your teacher colleagues and your site administrator about where you stand.

Questions:
1. You are aware of the need to maintain credibility with both your peers and your administrator. What will you say to them?
2. What are the ways in which you might successfully resolve this seemingly impossible situation?

Scenario 3: New Knowledge and What To Do with It

You have just returned from a national conference that featured some renowned figures in educational administration. You are anxious to share your experiences with your site administrator and the school faculty. The site administrator suggests that you make a short presentation at the next faculty meeting. During your presentation, you are confronted by questions about how the ideas you have presented can be operationalized at your school. You believe that you must respond to the questions or jeopardize the trust level you have so carefully been building, but you have not thought about ways of implementing the ideas.

Questions:
1. What will you do? Discuss your rationale.
2. Discuss the implications for your chosen course of action.

Scenario 4: Time and Priorities

You are feeling overwhelmed by your role as an administrative intern. You are being pressed to respond to responsibilities and obligations in your roles as spouse, parent, teacher, and student as well as intern. You realize that this experience is probably like the realities which will exist if you become a school administrator. You feel you must examine carefully ways in which to resolve this sense of being overwhelmed.

Questions:
1. What problems do you foresee if the sense of being overwhelmed is not addressed?
2. What are the implications for your relationship with significant others?
3. What support systems and resource bases do you have available? How can you elicit assistance?
4. How can you employ time management and prioritization skills?

THE ADVANCED STAGE

Scenario 1: Intern Group Closeness Is Threatened

This year's internship group has developed a strong support group. At least this was true until this spring, when three members of the group were offered principalships and five others were selected as assistant principals. The other twelve interns have also been looking for positions, but thus far without success. The group appears to be splintering into the "haves" and the "have nots," with what everyone feels is an unfortunate loss of the closeness and support that has developed over the year.

Questions:
1. Could this problem have been anticipated?
2. What kind of things might have been done earlier that would have helped in dealing with this problem?
3. What could still be done at this point in time to help restore the closeness that the group has developed?

Scenario 2: To Take the Job or Not to Take the Job

You have just completed your preparation program. The superintendent from your school district has been watching your progress, believes you are just the kind of person who should be appointed to the principalship that is available at Hill Top Elementary School, and has offered you the position. However, you have come to the conclusion that you would like to be a curriculum specialist. Ultimately you want to be an assistant superintendent for curriculum and instruction.

Questions:
1. How will you respond to the offer? Why?
2. What issues are involved in your decision in regard to the superintendent's offer? Provide a rationale for your answer.
3. Could you have avoided being in this situation?

Scenario 3: You and Your Mentor when It's Time to Leave

You and your site administrator have developed a close working relationship. In fact, he has gone well beyond the role requirements of a site administrator to become a mentor to you. His guidance, sponsorship, and support have helped you grow in many ways as an administrator and as a person. You are very conscious of this fact. Now, as the time approaches for you to bring your internship experience to a close, you begin to think seriously about the relationship you have had with your mentor.

Questions:
1. How can you let him know what his mentoring has meant to you?
2. Do you want the mentoring relationship to continue? If so, what do you anticipate it will be like?
3. Should you talk with your site administrator about your relationship and what further expectations, if any, each of you have about it?

Scenario 4: It's Over! What Have I Accomplished?

Your internship director has asked all of you to reflect on your experiences in the program. She is interested in knowing not only *what you have learned* but also *what changes you see in yourselves*. That's a tall order! You think it is a good idea, because so much has happened and you feel the need to get a perspective on it all.

Questions:
1. What approach should you take in reflecting about your experiences?
2. How can you get useful feedback from your fellow interns? From your site administrator? From others?
3. How can you bring it all together so that it makes sense?
4. How can you use the results of the effort to help you continue to grow as an educational administrator?

References

Allison, D. J. (1989, April). *Toward the fifth age: The continuing evolution of academic educational administration.* Paper presented at the annual meeting of the American Educational Research Association, San Francisco.

Anderson, G. (1988). *Practice as inquiry: The professional knowledge of the principal.* Unpublished document, Department of Educational Administration, University of New Mexico.

Anderson, M. E. (1989). Training and selecting school leaders. In S. C. Smith and P. K. Piele (Eds.), *School leadership* (pp. 53–84). Eugene, OR: ERIC Clearinghouse on Educational Management, University of Oregon.

Argyris, C., & Schön, D. (1974). *Theory in practice.* San Francisco: Jossey-Bass.

Bacilious, Z. (1987, March). *A proposal for the reconstruction of the administrative internship.* Papr presented at the annual meeting of the American Educational Research Association, Washington, D.C.

Backstrom, C. H., & Hursh, G. D. (1963). *Survey research.* Evanston, IL: Northwestern University Press.

Baltzell, C., & Dentler, R. (1983). *Selecting America's school principals: A sourcebook for educators.* Washington, DC: U.S. Department of Education, National Institute of Education.

Barnett, B., & Brill, A. (1988, October). *Building reflection into administrative training programs.* Paper presented at the annual convention of the University Council of Educational Administration, Cincinnati, OH.

Bennis, W. (1989). *On becoming a leader.* Reading, MA: Addison-Wesley.

Birren, J. (1987). The best of all stories. *Psychology Today, 22*(5), 91–92.

Bobroff, B., & Milstein, M. (1988, October). *Utilizing assessment centers for administrative internship selection.* Paper presented at the second annual convention of the University Council for Educational Administration, Cincinnati, OH.

Bova, B., & Phillips, R. (1984). Mentoring as a learning experience for adults. *Journal of Teacher Education, 35*(3), 16–20.

Boyer, E. L. (1983). *High schools: A report on secondary education in America.* New York: Harper & Row.

Briner, C. (1963). The role of internships in the total preparation program for educational administration: A frontier perspective. In S. Hencley (Ed.), *The internship in administrative preparation* (pp. 5–21). Columbus, OH: UCEA.

Carnegie Forum on Education and the Economy. (1986). *A nation prepared: Teachers for the 21st century.* New York: The Carnegie Foundation.

Conway, J. A., Jennings, R. E., & Milstein, M. M. (1974). *Understanding communities.* Englewood Cliffs, NJ: Prentice-Hall.

Cummings, K. (1989, April). *From Knowledge base to knowledge store: A move in the right direction?* Paper presented at the annual meeting of the American Educational Research Association, San Francisco.

Cunningham, L., & Nystrand, R. (1969). Toward greater relevance in preparation programs for urban school administrators. *Educational Administration Quarterly, 5*(1), 16–17.

Daresh, J. (1987, October). *Administrative internships and field experiences: A status report.* Paper presented at the annual meeting of the University Council of Educational Administration, Charlottesville, VA.

Daresh, J. (1988, April). *Are field based programs the answer to the reform of administrator preparation programs?* Paper presented at the annual meeting of the American Educational Research Association, New Orleans, LA.

Daresh, J., & Nestor, K. (1987). *Annotated bibliography on the use of field experience to train educational leaders* (UCEA project paper). Phoenix, AZ: University Council for Educational Administration, Center on Field Relations in Educational Administration Training Programs.

Denzin, N. (1978). *The research art: A theoretical introduction to sociological methods,* 2nd ed. New York: McGraw-Hill.

Department of Elementary School Principals. (1968). *The elementary principalship in 1968.* Washington, DC: National Education Association.

Duttweiler, P. C. (1988). *Organizing for excellence.* Austin, TX: Southwest Educational Development Laboratory.

Edmonds, R. (1979). Effective schools for the urban poor. *Educational Leadership, 37*(1), 15–24.

Fitz-Gibbon, C. T., & Morris, L. L. (1987). *Focus on evaluation.* Newbury Park, CA: Sage.

French, J., & Caplan, R. (1970). Psycho-social factors in coronary heart disease. *Industrial Medicine,* 383–397.

Frey, B., & Noller, R. (1983). Mentoring: A legacy of success. *The Journal of Creative Behavior, 17*(1), 60–64.

Good, C. V. (1966). *Essentials of educational research.* New York: Appleton-Century-Crofts.

Goodlad, J. I. (1983). *A place called school.* New York: McGraw-Hill.

Grady, M., Layton, J., & Bohling-Philipi, V. (1988). *Clinical experiences in educational administration, 1960–1987.* Tempe, AZ: University Council for Educational Administration.

Greenfield, W. (1985). The moral socialization of school administrators: Informal role learning outcomes. *Educational Administration Quarterly, 21*(4), 99–120.

Greenfield, W. (1987). Moral imagination and interpersonal competence and the work of school administrators. In N. J. Boyan (Ed.), *Handbook of research on educational administration* (pp. 207–232). New York: Longman.

Griffiths, D. (1988, April). *Educational administration reform: PDQ or RIP.* Paper presented at the annual meeting of the American Educational Research Association, New Orleans, LA.

Hazlett, J. (1986). School-university partnerships. *Contemporary education, 57,* 192–193.

Heller, R., & Conway, J. (1988, September). Who and what you are make you the pillar of the community. *The Executive Educator, 10*(9), 21–22.

Heller, R., Conway, J., & Jacobsen, S. (1988, September). Here is your blunt critique of administrator preparation. *Executive Educator, 10*(9), 18–21.

Hencley, S. P. (Ed.). (1963). *The internship in administrative preparation.* Washington, DC: The Committee for the Advancement of Educational Administration.

Jick, T. D. (1984). Mixing qualitative and quantitative methods: Triangulation in action. In T. S. Bateman & G. R. Ferris (Eds.), *Methods and analysis in organizational research* (pp. 364–372). Reston, VA: Reston Publishing Company.

Joyce, B. R., Hersh, R. H., & McKibbin, M. (1983). *The structure of school improvement.* New York: Longman.

Kolb, D. (1984). *Experiential learning: Experience as the source of learning and development.* Englewood Cliffs, NJ: Prentice-Hall.

Kouzes, J., & Posner, B. (1987). *The leadership challenge.* San Francisco: Jossey-Bass.

Land, A. (1988). Does college/school district collaboration work? Yes, with proper care! *AASA Professor, 11*(1), 9–11.

LaPlant, J. (1988, October). *An examination of clinical experiences in medical education: Considerations for the reform of field-based learning in administrator preparation programs.* Paper presented at the annual meeting of the University Council of Educational Administration, Cincinnati, OH.

LaPlant, J., Hill, J., Gallagher, K., & Wagstaff, L. (1989). Proactive recruitment and initial training experiences for potential administrators: Issues for administrator preparation. *AASA Professor, 11*(4), 8–12.

Lewis, A. (1989). *How to write a better resume.* New York: Baron's Educational Series.

Lieberman, A., & Miller, L. (1984). School improvement: Themes and variations. In A. Lieberman (Ed.), *Rethinking school improvement* (pp. 96–111). New York: Teachers College Press.

Likert, R. (1938). A technique for the measurement of attitudes. *Archives of Psychology, 140,* 73–78.

Lipnak, J., & Stamps, J. (1982). *Networking.* New York: Doubleday.

Malone, J. T. (1975). *Dress for success.* New York: Warner.

Malone, J. T. (1977). *The woman's dress for success book.* New York: Warner.

Mangieri, J. N. (Ed.). (1985). *Excellence in education.* Fort Worth: Texas Christian University Press.

Martin, M., & Kelly, C. (1989, October). *Expanding the knowledge base about the quality of administrator candidates: A retort to the policymakers and the national reports.* Paper presented at the University Council for Educational Administration, Phoenix, AZ.

McLeary, L., & Ogawa, R. (1985). Locating principals who are leaders: The assessment center concept. *Educational Considerations, 12*(3), 321–325.

Milstein, M. (1990). Rethinking the clinical aspects in administrative preparation: From theory to practice. In S. L. Jacobson & J. Conway (Eds.), *Educational leadership in an age of reform.* New York: Longman.

Milstein, M., & Bobroff, B. (1988). *The cooperative educational administration internship program.* Unpublished paper, University of New Mexico, Albuquerque.

Milstein, M., & Feidler, C. (1989). The status of and potential for administrator assessment centers in education. *Urban Education, 23*(4), 361–376.

Mitchell, R., & Kerchner, F. (1983). Labor relations and teacher policy. In L. S. Shulman & G. Sykes (Eds.), *Handbook of teaching and policy* (pp. 214–238). New York: Longman.

Murphy, J., & Hallinger, P. (1987). *Approaches in administrative training.* Albany: State University of New York Press.

Murphy, M., & Hart, A. (1989, April). *Preparing principals to lead in restructured schools.* Paper presented at the annual meeting of the American Educational Research Association, San Francisco.

Muse, I., Wasden, F., & Thomas, G. (1988). *The mentor principal handbook.* Provo, UT: Brigham Young University Leaders Preparation Program.

National Commission on Excellence in Education. (1983). *A nation at risk: The imperative for educational reform.* Washington, DC: U.S. Department of Education.

National Commission on Excellence in Educational Administration. (1987). *Leaders for America's schools.* Tempe, AZ: University Council for Educational Administration.

National Society for the Study of Education. (1964). *Behavioral science and educational administration.* Chicago: University of Chicago Press.

Nevo, D. (1983). The conceptualization of educational evaluation: An analytical review of the literature. *Review of Educational Research, 52*(1), 117–128.

Parker, Y. (1988). *The resume catalog: 200 damn good examples.* Berkeley: Ten Speed Press.

Parten, M. (1950). *Surveys, polls and samples.* New York: Harper & Row.

Phillips-Jones, L. (1983). *Mentors and proteges.* New York: Holt, Rinehart, & Winston.

Polanyi, M. (1958). *Personal knowledge.* Chicago: University of Chicago Press.

Richardson, S. A., Dowrehnwend, B. S., & Klein, D. (1965). *Interviewing.* New York: Basic Books.

Roche, G. (1979). Much ado about mentors. *Harvard Business Review, 57*(1), 14–28.

Rouche, J. E., & Baker, III, G. A. (1986). *Profiling excellence in America's schools.* Arlington, VA: American Association of School Administrators.

Schein, E. (1985). *Organizational culture and leadership.* San Francisco: Jossey-Bass.

Schön, D. (1983). *The reflective practitioner.* New York: Basic Books.

Schön, D. (1984). Leadership as reflection-in-action. In T. Sergiovanni & J. Corbally (Eds.), *Leadership and organizational culture* (pp. 36–63). Chicago: University of Illinois Press.

Sergiovanni, T. (1984). Leadership and excellence in schooling. *Educational Leadership,* 4–13.

Sergiovanni, T., & Corbally, J. (1984). *Leadership and organizational culture.* Chicago: University of Illinois Press.

Short, P., & Ashbaugh, C. (1988, October). *The administrative internship: A problemsolving experience.* Paper presented at the annual meeting of the University Council of Educational Administration, Cincinnati, OH.

Skalski, J., Lohman, M., Szcepanik, J., Baratta, A., Bacilious, Z., & Schulte, S. (1987, April). *Administrative internships.* Paper presented at the Annual Meeting of the American Educational Research Association, Washington, DC.

Smith, M. (1987). *The resume writer's handbook.* New York: Barnes and Noble.

Spady, W. G., & Marx, G. (1984). *Excellence in our schools: Making it happen.* Arlington, VA: American Association of School Administrators, Far West Laboratory for Educational Research and Development.

Stager, M., & Leithwood, K. (1988, April). *Cognitive flexibility and inflexibility in principal's problem solving.* Paper presented at the annual meeting of the American Educational Research Association, New Orleans, LA.

Stecher, B. M., & Davis, W. A. (1987). *How to focus an evaluation.* Newbury Park, CA: Sage.

Swoboda, M., & Miller, S. (1986). Networking and mentoring: Career strategy of women in academic administration. *Journal of the National Association of Women Deans, 50*(1), 8–13.

Wayson, W. W., Mitchell, B., Pinell, G. S., & Landis, D. (1988). *Up from excellence: The impact of the excellence movement on schools.* Bloomington, IN: Phi Delta Kappa Educational Foundation.

Webster's new collegiate dictionary. (1981). Springfield, MA: Merriam.

Wheaton, G. A. (1950). *A status study of internship programs in school administration.* New York: Teachers College, Columbia University.

Wu, P. (1986). Lessons for collaboration between educational agencies. *Journal of Teacher Education, 37*(5), 61–64.

Yates, M. (1988). *Resumes that knock 'em dead.* Holbrook, MA: Adams.

Index

Field supervisors, *continued*
  personal attributes of, 21–23
  professional experience of, 23
  professional reputations of, 23
  selection and recruitment of, 21–23
  in working relationships with site adminis-
    trators and interns, 67
Financial arrangements, 35
Fitz-Gibbon, C. T., 112
French, J., 55
Frey, B., 72

Gallagher, K., 73
Gender
  job placement and, 89
  respect for differences in, 18
Good, C. V., 112
Goodlad, J. I., 1, 70
Graduate seminars, internship programs pro-
    moted in, 42
Grady, M., 6
Greenfield, W., 52–53
Gresso, Donn W., ix
Griffiths, D., 3

Hallinger, P., 3–4, 51–52
Hart, A., 70
Harvard University, 4
Hazlett, J., 74, 79
Heller, R., 3, 89, 91–92
Hencley, S. P., 4–5
Hersh, R. H., 2, 70
Hill, J., 73
Human skills, 53
Hursh, G. D., 112

Intellectual knowledge, 5
Interns. *See also* Cohorts, intern
  clinical activities for. *See* Clinical experi-
    ences and activities
  competency contracts with, 76–79
  in determining program approach, 36
  evaluation of. *See* Evaluations of interns
  expectations surveys for, 133–134
  in field experience planning, 61
  in identification and development of
    knowledge base, 56
  and national groups and organizations to
    become familiar with, 131–132

as participants in design and conduct of
    programs, 37, 39, 41
partnership roles and responsibilities of,
    72–73
selection and recruitment of. *See* Selection
    and recruitment of interns
in working relationships with school dis-
    tricts and colleges, 66–79
in working relationships with site adminis-
    trators and field supervisors, 67
Internship, source of term, 4
Internship programs
  advertising availability of, 28
  demand for, 1–8
  emphases of, 6
  priorities of, 29
  purposes of, 6–8
Interviews
  in evaluations, 112
  in intern selection process, 43–44
  for jobs, 97–99
  in selecting and recruiting program direc-
    tors, 20

Jacobsen, S., 3
Jennings, R. E., 112, 114
Jick, T. D., 112
Job placement, 83–100
  alumni evaluation of, 135–138
  and applying for positions, 96–100
  appropriate attire and, 97
  and assessing career directions, 84–86
  assessing readiness for, 29, 83, 106–107,
    110
  assessment centers in, 99–100
  and career planning, 83–87
  and certification and licensure, 93
  compensation in, 91–92
  demographics in, 89–91
  and finding right job, 87–93
  and getting paperwork in order, 93–96
  interviewing skills and, 97–99
  kinds of positions available in, 88–89
  networking in, 86–87
  philosophy/purposes/platform in, 95–96
  references and, 96
  résumés and, 93–95
  sources of administrative positions in, 92–
    93

About the Authors

MIKE M. MILSTEIN, Professor of Educational Administration, the University of New Mexico, played a key role in the development of that department's innovative approaches to administrative internships. Prior to this position, he was a professor of educational administration at SUNY/Buffalo. His teaching, research, and writing interests are in the area of organization development. Most recently he has focused his energies on the extent to which educators are experiencing plateauing in their work lives.

BETTYE M. BOBROFF received her Ph.D. from the University of Texas at Austin after serving the Albuquerque Public Schools as a practicing administrator. She subsequently joined the faculty at the University of New Mexico and was instrumental in developing and implementing the Cooperative Educational Administration Internship Program. At present she is the Director of Instruction at Bernalillo Public Schools, Bernalillo, New Mexico.

L. NAN RESTINE is an Assistant Professor in Educational Leadership at Western Kentucky University, Bowling Green, Kentucky. She received her Ph.D. from the University of New Mexico and served as the Assistant Director of the Cooperative Educational Administration Internship Program. Her research interests are focused in the areas of adult development, experiential learning, and the professional preparation of educators.